ALSATIANS

This handbook is not written for the experienced fancier, but is intended for the guidance of the pet dog owner who is anxious to give his dog the proper care and attention which he needs, and to assist him in obtaining the maximum amount of pleasure in the ownership of one of the most beautiful and intelligent of all dogs.

ALSATIANS

BY

LILLIAN LEONARD

FOYLES HANDBOOKS

LONDON

ISBN 0 7071 0608 7

Reprinted 1971
Revised edition 1972
Reprinted 1973
Reprinted 1974
Reprinted 1976
Reprinted 1977
Reprinted 1978
Reprinted 1979

Published in Great Britain by
W. & G. Foyle Ltd.,
125 Charing Cross Road,
London WC2H 0EB

Printed and bound in Great Britain
at The Pitman Press, Bath

CONTENTS

CHAPTER 1

HISTORY OF THE BREED

ALSATIANS (German Shepherd Dogs) are truly international. They are to be seen in every part of the world and are prized above all other breeds for their exceptional sagacity and for the protection and companionship they afford to their owners living in isolated places. Yet at the same time, they fit readily into the pattern of town life. No breed of dog is possessed of a keener sense of hearing, nor with that uncanny sixth sense of knowing when danger is near. They are always on the alert and ready to give the alarm whenever necessary, and their highly developed protective instincts make them ideal guard dogs and companions for children.

Although fairly large in size, they are seldom clumsy, and are especially devoid of any 'doggy' smell, which makes them ideal house dogs. They are not aggressive in nature, and will seldom fight unless driven to it. They are 'One man Dogs' and do not readily make friends with strangers, but will tolerate them if needs be. They are never so happy as when carrying out their master's commands, they thrive on being made to do do things, and are at their very worst if kept confined in kennels without human companionship.

Despite the many conflicting stories told about their origin, including the fallacy that they have wolf blood, the Alsatian breed is a very pure and ancient one. They are descended from the native sheep dogs of Germany, and unlike many modern breeds of dog which have been 'manufactured' by man by crossing one breed with another, the Alsatian has remained a pure type, possessing primitive, natural beauty, free from exaggeration of any kind.

It is during the past fifty to sixty years that the Alsatian has become a show breed. A German cavalry officer named von Stephanitz became interested in the improvement of the breed, and it was he who was responsible for the formation of the first club in 1899 (named The Verein fur Deutsche Schaferhund) (S.V.). This club started the stud book, and drew up the Standard of Points for the breed. The German standard has been adopted all over the world and in the fifty years which have passed since it was drawn up, it has been varied only in the very smallest points. The whole standard is based on the dog being essentially a working dog, capable of great endurance and adaptable to any climate.

In all probability, the breed would never have been known in England to any extent, and certainly not by the name 'Alsatian' had it not been for the 1914–18 war. Prior to this, the Germans has used the breed mainly as sheep dogs, but with the outbreak of war, they trained large numbers of them to work with their army as Messenger Dogs, and carriers of Red Cross supplies to the wounded. It was some of these working dogs, found or captured by the British forces, which were brought back to England after the war, which were founders of this ever-popular breed in England.

To the British dog-loving public, they were something entirely new. Their great beauty, intelligence and aptitude for being trained, very soon placed them amongst the most popular breeds. Those people responsible for introducing them to this country were faced with a problem as to what name the breed should be given. Their correct name of 'German Shepherd Dog', so soon after hostilities had ceased, might well have prejudiced people against them. After much deliberation they were registered at The Kennel Club as 'The Alsatian Wolfdog'; totally incorrect, but arrived at because many of the early specimens came from the borders of Germany and Alsace Lorraine and were known by the colloquial name of 'Chien Loup' because they resembled the wolf in colour and possessed erect ears. This remained their official name for many years, but eventually the 'Wolfdog' was dropped. Their registered name is now 'The Alsatian' (German Shepherd Dog), although for all ordinary purposes they are just 'Alsatians'.

Their sudden rise to popularity, from being practically unknown to the second most popular breed, all in a matter of a few years, led to a great deal of commercial breeding and attracted many unscrupulous 'exploiters' of the breed. So great was the demand for puppies, and so little was known about the correct points of the breed by the man in the street, that anything which could be called an Alsatian found a ready market. Little attention was paid by many breeders to the proper upbringing and mental development of this highly intelligent breed, as long as they could be sold at high prices, and it was inevitable that many nervous and unreliable specimens were bred and sold. There were also many imported from the Continent: some good, but many of poor quality.

A great deal of the publicity given to the breed in the daily press was due to the world-wide appeal made by 'Rin Tin Tin' and 'Strongheart' the two wonder dogs of the films. Alsatians became 'news' and their doings both good and bad were reported, until in the middle 1920s, a press attack was launched against the breed which very nearly brought about its end. Grossly exaggerated stories were published in an endeavour to prove that the breed was savage and unreliable, and closely related to the wolf, and it was due to the untiring efforts of a few members of 'The Alsatian League' that many of the false stories were disproved.

The temporary setback had the good result of eliminating the commercial breeder who could no longer make easy profits, and a new era was started by the genuine lovers of this wonderful breed which had survived such an unfair press campaign. Breeders set to work to repair the damage done, paying special attention to the temperament of their breeding stock, and to the correct training and upbringing of their puppies. Obedience classes were started and became extremely popular. Small local clubs were formed all over England where the correct methods of training were taught.

The Kennel Club approved the schedule of exercises to be carried out at Working Trials, and granted the titles of 'Working Trial Champion', 'Utility Dog' and 'Companion Dog,' etc., to those dogs which qualified at trials. So it was that the Alsatian breed became established, not only as one of the most popular show and companion breeds, but also as the pioneer working breed.

At the outbreak of the second World War in 1939, there was a nation-wide appeal for trained dogs and experienced trainers. They were needed to work with the Royal Air Force and the Army, and a large number of Alsatians and their trainers were enlisted to form the first Government Guard Dog School ever known in Great Britain.

These early recruits, mostly amateur owners who had learned training in their spare time, were soon able to pass on their knowledge to others in the armed forces. Large numbers of Alsatians were lent by their owners for the duration of the war to be trained for useful purposes. They performed invaluable service to the country, and saved an enormous number of lives when working with paratroopers, in mine detection, and with the rescue parties in the Civil Defence. They also guarded aerodromes and munition depots.

CHAPTER 2

CHOOSING A PUPPY

If you are buying a puppy with the intention of keeping it for the rest of its life, it never pays to be in too great a hurry. Nearly all puppies are delightful, helpless little creatures with appealing eyes, but you must remember, they do not always remain so.

Before buying a pedigree puppy, you should learn as much as you can about the breed, its general characteristics, etc. Find out what a healthy puppy should weigh for its age, and satisfy yourself that the puppy you are considering is a normal specimen of the breed.

Price is not always any criterion of quality, but you must bear in mind that the initial cost of a puppy is only a fraction of what it is going to cost by the time it is fully grown, and it therefore pays to buy the best obtainable. It costs just as much, or often more, to rear a poor specimen as a good one, so it will pay you every time to go to a reputable breeder and pay a fair price for a properly bred and properly reared specimen.

A safe guide is to inspect the parents, for there is obviously a better chance that puppies bred from sound, healthy and typical parents will themselves be better specimens than those bred from faulty parent stock. I do not advise anyone to take delivery of an Alsatian puppy under eight weeks of age. They need the warmth and protection of the mother and other puppies in the litter up to this age, and to take them away to live alone at an earlier age is merely putting an unnecessary strain on the puppy, and adding to the work of rearing it.

Make sure that the puppy is clean and free from vermin or skin disorder, paying special attention to the skin on the belly and the inside of the shoulders. Any inflammation or spots on these parts should be viewed with suspicion. When picked up, the puppy should feel firm and solid, but the skin should be loose. The legs should be straight and strong, with elbows fitting close to the body. The bones of the legs should appear big and out of proportion to the size of the puppy, for these always 'fine down'. The large knee bones of an Alsatian puppy are often mistaken by the inexperienced as being a sign of rickets. These large knee joints disappear as the puppy develops. The body should be deep and solid; in a young puppy there should be little sign of 'waist', but on the other hand, the belly should not appear distended. The latter is either a sign of unsuitable feeding or of worms.

The formation of the shoulders and hindquarters can, to some extent, be judged on quite a young puppy. The best way of judging, is to see the puppies running free, when those with well angulated shoulders and hindquarters will move with greater freedom and with a longer stride.

I do not recommend anyone to buy a puppy with over large or heavy, leathery ears, especially if they are wide set and carried at the side of the head. This type of ear is slower in stiffening to the typical erect position, and in quite a small percentage of cases they remain soft and the dog does not appear to be a typical specimen of his breed. It is far safer to choose a puppy with smaller ears carried in a somewhat erratic manner, for this means the beginning of movements towards becoming erect. It is not at all unusual for a puppy which has already had its ears erect, to drop them during the process of teething, but there is no cause for alarm on this account; they invariably become erect again when the teething period is over.

The colour of the eye in young puppies is rather difficult to determine, but those with very light yellow-coloured eyes are not desirable. A soft brown eye always gives a kinder and more pleasing expression.

The coat should be shiny and lie flat on the body. A staring coat often denotes worms or lack of condition. Long-coated specimens are often to be found in predominantly smooth-coated litters. There is a distinct difference, both in the length and texture of the hair. In long-coated specimens the hair is usually much softer with a wavy look down the spine, and a fluffy appearance round the ears.

Colour should be of secondary importance, except in the case of white or cream which are not desirable. All else being equal, it is advisable to choose a puppy with rich pigmentation and not one which has faded or is of indefinite colouring. In sables or greys, there should be darker markings, and a black muzzle is preferable to a light one, the latter gives a foxy appearance and detracts from the expression. Black and tans should be rich and deep in colour, with not too much light hair in proportion to black.

With the change of the puppy coat, the light markings tend to increase and spread. So it is better to choose one with a large black saddle. Sables and greys often get darker when *the second* coat appears, this is because the second coat is usually tipped with black not found in the puppy coat.

All young puppies are inclined to carry their tails up when at play, but do not choose a puppy which constantly carries its tail above the level of its back, or in a curl or hook at the tip. A puppy which tucks its tail between its legs is a nervous one and will need a lot of extra care in its upbringing. It is far better to choose a puppy which runs towards you with confidence and trust than one which hangs back and has to be coaxed into making friends.

The feet, like the knees, of young puppies appear large and rather out of proportion. They should be round and the toes well arched and the nails should be short and black in colour.

It is most important to examine the mouth. The teeth of the upper and lower jaw should meet with the upper slightly overlapping, but touching the lower. If the upper jaw protrudes in front of the lower jaw it is termed 'overshot', and if the lower jaw protrudes in front of the upper jaw it is 'undershot'. Both are extremely bad faults.

Do not choose a puppy with dew claws left on the hind legs. These should be removed when about five days old.

Cleanliness being of the utmost importance in the rearing of puppies, a properly reared and properly housed puppy should smell sweet and clean. From their very earliest days puppies will be clean in their habits and will never foul their beds if they are given the opportunity of using another place. One should always be suspicious about any puppy which has a dirty coat or has an unpleasant smell, for dirtiness encourages germs and vermin.

Always enquire whether the puppy has been treated for worms. This is routine in all well-run kennels, but sometimes neglected by careless or irresponsible breeders. Every puppy should have had its first worm medicine at five to seven weeks, and it is most inadvisable to take delivery of a puppy until after this has been done. No amount of care or good feeding will be of value until the puppy has been freed of worms, and there is no doubt that many more puppies die in the early stages from worms than from disease.

Make certain before purchasing a pedigree puppy that all particulars relating to its pedigree are in order. If the breeder is unknown to you, insist on taking the pedigree with the puppy, and remember that to be eligible for Class I registration at The Kennel Club, *both* parents must be registered, so be careful to see that their registration numbers are shown on the puppy's pedigree. If the breeder has already registered the puppy, it will carry that name for the rest of its life and you will need a Kennel Club transfer form signed by the breeder in order that the puppy can be transferred and recorded as your property. This is specially important, as no dog can be exhibited which is not duly transferred to the name of the exhibitor and in the case of a bitch which is bred from, the official breeder of her litter is the person in whose name she is registered at the time of whelping, so make sure that she has been transferred *prior* to whelping. On the other hand, if the puppy has *not* been registered by the breeder, you should make a point of getting a Kennel Club form for registration signed by the breeder before you take delivery of the puppy. You are then able to choose your own name for it, and get it registered in your own name, in the first instance, when no transfer will be necessary.

A great many disputes could be avoided if the purchaser insists on the foregoing formalities being carried out at the time of purchase.

Both registration and transfer forms are obtainable free from The Kennel Club, 1–4 Clarges Street, Piccadilly, London, W.1.

CHAPTER 3

PUPPY REARING AND TRAINING

BEFORE purchasing a puppy, the prospective owner should make certain that he has all the facilities for properly housing it, and the time needed for correct feeding and exercising. It is far better if *one* person is able to undertake the care of the puppy in the early days. A daily routine should be worked out and strictly kept, and meals must be given at regular intervals.

It is not fair to any puppy to take it from the seclusion of a kennel where it has been able to rely upon the protection of its mother and brothers and sisters, and to expect that puppy to be anything but lonely and a little difficult for the first few days. It will miss the competition of eating against others at meal times and may need a good deal of coaxing to get it to eat alone. But remember, in those first few days, you can establish a relationship between yourself and the puppy which will be lasting. You can teach him to trust and rely upon you not only for his food and other bodily needs, but also for affection and companionship. This he will badly need in the early days, and the more time you can spend with him the better.

It is never too early to start simple training. The difference between right and wrong can be indicated by the tone of your voice —nothing more than that is necessary with a sensitive breed such as Alsatians, but the praise or scolding must be instant or it is useless. A puppy has a very short memory, and it is quite senseless to scold it for something which it has already done. The right way is to watch him, and try to catch him in the act of doing something which is not allowed, then your correction will be associated in his mind with this act. The next time, if you apply the same correction in the same manner, the puppy will remember and your first battle has been won.

Always be very lavish with your praise and rewards in the early stages of training and use commands which are short and simple, for instance 'Sit' and not 'Sit down'; 'Come', and not 'Come here'. The fewer words you ask the puppy to remember, the better. Always remember that encouragement applied at the right moment is just as lasting as correction, and the great thing in all training is to keep your puppy happy and to maintain his trust in you.

HOUSE TRAINING

If your puppy has been purchased from a good kennel, he will have received some preliminary training whilst still in the nest. As soon as the puppies are old enough to run about, and the mother finds the process of 'cleaning up' the excreta is getting a little beyond her, the puppies can be taught to use one corner of their kennel as their 'lavatory'. Always place them in this same spot after meals and when they first wake up after sleep. Cover this spot with newspapers, or a metal tray sprinkled with sawdust, leaving a little of their excreta there to start with, and you will find that the puppies will automatically go back to the same spot, and you will very rarely find their sleeping bed is made foul.

The newspapers are easy to replace, or the tray cleaned. This early training in the nest teaches the puppy to have a proper place in which to relieve nature, and when he is old enough to go away to his new home, your first task is to divert that instinct to be clean, towards the place which is to be his in the new home. Keep putting him out to the same spot whenever he looks in danger of misbehaving, stay with him using gentle words of encouragement, and remember, that the 'danger periods' are always just after meals and when first waking up after sleep.

The moment he 'obliges' in the right spot, pick him up, and make a tremendous fuss of him, and carry him back into the house. It is quite useless and cruel to punish a puppy for making a mess *after* it has happened, your only time for correction is if you catch him *at the time*. By giving him opportunities, and exercising patience, you will quickly teach him to be clean during the day. The great thing is never to leave him running about by himself in the house when you cannot spend the time to watch him. Bring him into the house for short periods only, when he can be kept under observation, and put him out the very moment he shows signs of uneasiness. Avoid the necessity for scolding, by anticipating his needs, and if, by this treatment you can prevent him making messes in the house, there is less likelihood of his going back to the same spot and repeating his misbehaviour.

It is unreasonable to expect a young puppy to go all through the night without relieving nature, so he must be put to sleep in a place where he can have his tray of sawdust or newspapers, and it will help if you make a practice of putting him out as late as possible at night, and very early in the morning.

CHAPTER 4

FEEDING

CAREFULLY regulated feeding is necessary for dogs of all ages, but especially for puppies. When puppies are first weaned, 'little and often' should be your guide. From five to nine weeks they will need feeding five times per day at about four-hourly intervals. Overfeeding at any one meal will merely distend their small stomachs and cause indigestion. The diet should be well balanced to contain all the necessary vitamins, and must contain a high proportion of protein, for you must remember puppies should gain weight at the rate of approximately half a pound per day, and will eventually grow into dogs weighing seventy-five to ninety pounds. The greater part of this growth will take place in the first year of the puppy's life, and it is never possible to make up for growth lost during this vital period. Your object must be to grow bone, and to maintain stamina, and it is only by correct feeding that you can do this. Good, healthy condition is the best insurance against minor illnesses, and even if the puppy is unlucky enough to contract some infectious disease, there is far more chance of successfully nursing him through it, if he was well nourished to start with, for he will have reserve flesh and strength to fall back upon. Nowadays, most common dog diseases of the infectious type can be largely prevented by inoculation.

From three to four months of age, your puppy will need as much food as when he is fully grown.

The following is a well-balanced diet for a puppy from eight to twelve weeks.

7-8 a.m.—Half to 1 pint of warm milk thickened with arrowroot, semolina, or breakfast cereal. Sweeten with glucose or sugar. Crush and mix into it two Calcium tablets.

11 a.m.—Half pound of good quality lean meat, minced or cut up finely. Mix with wholemeal rusk or puppy biscuit meal which has been scalded with good gravy made from bones and vegetables.

Never make the meal too sloppy, but give as dry as possible. The quantity of rusk or biscuit must depend upon the appetite of the puppy; the meat is of far more importance.

After the meal has been eaten, give one cod liver oil capsule. It is far safer to give the cod liver oil in capsule form than mixing the liquid form in the food, as this will sometimes put the puppy off eating it, and then the whole meal is wasted. You are also certain that the right amount has been given.

2 p.m.—Another milky meal similar to the early morning meal. Give another two Calcium tablets as before.

6 p.m.—Another meal with half pound of meat with gravy and puppy meal or rusk, as at 11 a.m.

9-10 p.m.—Warm milk with a raw egg beaten into it. (At eight weeks, the puppy will need only half an egg at this meal, but by the time it is twelve weeks old, the quantity can have been gradually increased until it is having the whole egg at this meal.)

At twelve weeks the number of meals can be reduced to four per day, cutting out one of the milky meals and gradually increasing the amount of meat. From then onwards the amount given at each meal can be gradually increased, and the number of meals reduced.

At six months it is only necessary to feed three times per day, and at one year twice per day. Adults are best fed just once per day.

From the time the puppy is six months old until fully mature, it will need 1½ to 2 lbs. of meat per day. Care must be taken when giving cod liver, or halibut oil, as too much will often cause digestive trouble. The refined types sold for human use are far better and safer than the cruder types made for animals. Calcium tablets are much easier to give if crushed to a powder. Occasionally, fish can be given as an alternative to meat, but it must be cooked. Meat is best given raw, but it can be cooked with vegetables as a change.

Never give small bones of any sort which can be swallowed.

Rabbit and poultry bones are especially dangerous, and under no circumstances should they be allowed. Large beef bones such as shin bones can be safely given, and are often helpful during the teething period. Gnawing at large bones will often strengthen the muscles running up to the ears, and will assist the ears in becoming erect.

Always see that there is a bowl of fresh water available to the dog, and keep it in the same place so that the dog knows where to find it.

CHAPTER 5

BREEDING

To the genuine dog lover, breeding is the most satisfactory part of dog keeping. It provides a never ending source of interest, and no matter whether it is a fancier with years of experience, or the absolute novice, there is always the incentive and opportunity to improve, and to benefit by past success or failure.

The forces of nature tend to work against cultivation in all spheres of living things. Just as everything in the flower and vegetable world will revert to the wild plant from which it sprang, if left untended and uncultivated, so it is in the animal world. It is only by careful, selective breeding that one can hope to improve, and more important still, to maintain that improvement. 'Like begets like,' is a true saying up to a point, but there is more in it than just mating two animals of similar type to breed progeny as good or better than themselves. These similar parents must have behind them ancestors with good qualities in order to be able to transmit them. Furthermore, the parent stock must be suited to each other, and have compensating qualities.

Space does not permit the expounding of the scientific theories of breeding, but the careful study of pedigrees, and knowing the qualities which the various dogs in the pedigree were known to transmit, helps a lot in selecting the most suitable animals to mate together. How often one hears the boast that 'my dog has X number of champions in his pedigree' the inference being, that because of this, he *must* be a good dog. If that were the case, how easy the whole matter of breeding would be.

It is no more certain that champions mated together will produce better stock than any others, unless they have the blood which suits. If the animal you wish to breed from has a fault, you can set about trying to breed out that fault by choosing a mate which excels where yours fails, but in doing this, take care not to introduce another equally bad fault in your effort to eliminate one.

If you find that the resulting litter shows an improvement, you cannot afford to be content, for you must always remember that these puppies still carry a tendency in their blood to the faults of the parents, even though they may not be obvious to the eye, and it will take further generations of selective breeding before the faults which you set out to eliminate have disappeared, and even then you will get the occasional 'throw back' to the faulty ancestor.

For the small breeder, the choice of the brood bitch is of paramount importance. The best type of bitch for breeding is one with good all-round qualities rather than one with exaggeration in one direction and failings in another. The sound bitch with no serious constructional weaknesses is far less of a gamble, for you can choose her mate from all the stud dogs in the country, and in a breed as numerous as the Alsatian, it should not be difficult to find a dog suitable both in structure and blood lines. If the first mating proves to be a disappointment, you will know what points need special consideration when you next select the sire. If, on the other hand, you are lucky enough to breed a really first-class litter at the first attempt, and you are satisfied that the puppies are a distinct improvement on the parent stock (when they have reached an age when it is possible to judge), it is probably a safer thing to repeat the same mating than to try out a different sire the next time, which may not suit your bitch so well. The breeding life of a bitch is too short to allow for a great deal of experiment, for it is never advisable to breed from an Alsatian bitch before her third season (usually at about two years of age), and she should not be mated more than once each year. Too frequent litters lower the stamina of the dam, and in each successive litter the puppies deteriorate.

The best way to gradually improve your stock is to keep the best bitch puppy of each litter as far as you can, or at least retain an interest in them, and then, when the time comes for them to be mated you will have an intimate knowledge of the parents as your guide in the choice of the sire. In this way you can build up a family based on your original brood bitch.

Broadly speaking, very close *inbreeding*, i.e., father to daughter—mother to son, brothers and sisters—or even half brothers and sisters, is not to be recommended as a general practice, although it is occasionally resorted to in order to fix certain characteristics much desired. But there are too many drawbacks to this method of breeding, notably loss of stamina and resistance to disease, and also a tendency to nervousness.

Just as inbreeding will fix good qualities, it will also fix faults which may take generations to breed out. A far safer system is that of *line breeding* which is still a method of fixing points, without the risks of close inbreeding. By this method, you mate animals of similar blood, but transmitted through different branches of the same family, and at the same time introducing some outside blood. A good example is the pedigree of English champion 'Quixotic of Huesca' which shows strong line breeding to 'Pericles av Hvitsand', a son of the famous bitch 'Quella of Brittas' who was also the dam of 'CH. Daga of Templefields', Thus we have four lines to this bitch 'Quella' in four generations, i.e., with the other four lines unrelated.

PEDIGREE OF CH. QUIXOTIC OF HUESCA

SIRE Quixotic of Isk	Galahad of Templefields	*Pericles av Hvitsand* (son of Quella)
		Ch. Daga of Templefields (daughter of Quella)
	Laetitia of Isk	*Pericles av Hvitsand* (son of Quella)
		Gloriole of Isk
DAM Danae of Huesca	Ch. Danko v Menkenmoor of Hardwick	Gr. Ch. Lex v Prussenblut
		Bionda v.d. Buchenhohe
	Aurora of Isk	*Pericles av Hvitsand* (son of Quella)
		Letton Alicia

Just as when inbreeding, care must be taken in line breeding not to perpetuate bad faults as well as the good points of the foundation stock, so it is obviously only worth while line-breeding to first-class animals.

Out Crossing is when two animals of different blood are mated together. The only real merit of such breeding is to increase stamina and virility, or when the danger line has been reached in line or inbreeding. After a suitable out-cross, it is then safe, as a rule, to go back to the original strain in the next generation.

Animals which are the result of repeated outcrossing cannot be relied upon to transmit their own characteristics with any regularity.

THE CARE OF THE BROOD BITCH AND HER LITTER

The preparation of a bitch for maternal duties should begin months before she is actually mated. She must be fed, and above all, exercised, so that she is in the very peak of condition when the time comes.

No Alsatian bitch should be mated before her third season; by which time she should have reached maturity. It will be fairly easy to calculate the time when you will want to have everything ready for the mating, by adding six months to the commencement of her last season. Your aim should be to have her in hard, rather lean condition, for this will mean that she will be able to carry her puppies with the minimum amount of strain, and the actual process of whelping will be far easier.

If you mate a bitch when she is too fat and soft, there is far more chance of her 'missing' and if she does prove in whelp, the weight of her own excessive fat, plus the puppies will be a great strain on her back. It will therefore be far more difficult to keep her properly exercised during the period of gestation, which is the secret of natural, easy whelping.

All bitches should be properly dosed for worms well before the expected time for mating and although it is never possible to completely eradicate the presence of worms in puppies, the risk can be enormously reduced by freeing the dam of these pests prior to mating.

Keep a close watch for the first signs or the bitch coming 'on heat'. There will be a discharge of blood from the vagina which will usually last about fourteen days, and during this time the vagina will swell.

The actual day for mating varies with each individual bitch, but there is roughly a period from the tenth to the eighteenth day when the bitch will be ready to accept the dog. The ideal time is generally thought to be immediately after the coloured discharge had ceased. If, when you pass your hand over the hindquarters of the bitch, she raises her tail to one side, this is the surest sign that she is ready for the stud dog.

For every reason, it is far better to take the bitch yourself to the stud dog if it is at all possible. She is far more likely to mate willingly if you are there to hold her yourself, and she is far less likely to be upset by the journey if you have accompanied her.

A maiden or nervous bitch will in some cases never show willingness at any period, and in this case, she should be introduced to the dog a day or so before the expected day for mating so that she can become accustomed to his attentions and overcome her fears. It is always a wise thing to choose an experienced stud dog to mate with a maiden or nervous bitch, for you are far more likely to get a satisfactory mating if the dog can be relied upon to perform his duty unaided, and in the least possible time.

Make certain that the bitch has been made thoroughly comfortable prior to the mating. Ensure that her bowels have been open that morning by giving her a tablespoonful of liquid paraffin the night before, and allow plenty of time to give her a good run before you introduce her to the dog. It is best to keep the bitch on a lead, and the dog should be introduced to her gradually and gently. If he is of an excitable nature, he is also best kept on a lead to start with, or the bitch may be put off by his too energetic attentions before she is ready to stand to him.

When the dog has penetrated the vagina there will be a 'tie' and this can last just a few minutes, or as long as thirty to forty minutes, and during the whole of this period it is advisable to keep the bitch standing as still as possible, and on a short lead, or she may try to throw herself to the ground and so injure the dog. As soon as the tie is over, take the bitch straight back to the house or kennel, and try to prevent her passing water for a while. She should be allowed time to settle down and rest before she is sent on a journey.

It is of the utmost importance to keep the bitch shut away from dogs for ten to fourteen days *after* she has been mated, for there is always a danger that she will be more willing to mate again after the original mating, and there have been many cases of bitches producing two litters by different sires within a few days of each other.

The full period of gestation is sixty-three days from the date of mating, but it is not at all unusual for Alsatian bitches to whelp two or three days early, so preparations must be made accordingly. It is always advisable to make arrangements with a qualified veterinary surgeon to be on call in case of need.

For the first week or two after mating, the bitch can be given her normal diet and exercise. Avoid fattening foods and ensure a well-balanced diet with plenty of good meat and vitamins such as cod liver oil, given in proper doses. From the fourth week onwards the amount of food should be gradually increased, and it is best divided into two or three meals per day so as to avoid any distension of the stomach. A milky meal can be introduced, and by the fifth week it is usually possible to tell whether the bitch is in whelp, especially if there is to be a large litter.

Gentle and regular exercise is of the utmost importance during the whole period of gestation.

Make all preparations well in advance, and introduce the bitch to the place where you want her to whelp, and let her feed and sleep there so that she is thoroughly used to it. A quiet, well-ventilated out-building or kennel is best, but free from draughts. It must be well away from the noise and distraction of other dogs, and it must be big enough to allow for a whelping box large enough for the bitch to lie stretched out at her full length. The sides of the whelping box need to be high enough to keep the puppies in, but low enough for the bitch to step out when she wishes to relieve nature, for she will never foul the bed where the puppies are.

It is necessary to have the whelping kennel well lighted in case the whelping should take place at night, but I must warn against the use of paraffin or other lighting or heating lamps which can be upset and cause fire.

As the time for whelping draws near, keep the bitch under constant observation and note anything unusual in her behaviour. It is not at all uncommon for bitches to go off their food during the last few days, and it may be necessary to spoil them with tempting morsels which they fancy. With the arrival of the puppies, the appetite will return, but it is important beforehand to keep up her spirits and strength for the strain of whelping.

From the first signs of uneasiness, the bitch should not be left alone, and the veterinary surgeon should be warned in case his help is needed. A normal, healthy bitch will do all that is necessary herself, but there is always the risk of complicated births. By staying with her, it is often possible to save the life of a puppy which might otherwise get pushed on one side or crushed during the birth of another puppy. One can also encourage the newly-born pups to breathe by blowing into their nostrils if they appear limp, and they can be gently guided to the mother's teats for suckling. Unless the whole process of whelping has been observed, it is not possible to know if the afterbirth has come away, for the bitch will usually devour this, and it is not until this has taken place that one can be certain that the whelping is finished.

During the process of whelping, the bitch should be disturbed as little as possible, she should be offered drinks of tepid milk with glucose in between the births. Never allow strangers or other dogs to come near, as this will have a very unsettling effect on the bitch, and may even cause her to destroy the puppies. Examine each puppy as it is born, handling it as little as possible. Any puppy with any deformity should be taken away and destroyed at once, but take care to do this without the bitch noticing.

Wait until the whelping is over and all the pups are safely gathered round the teats, and suckling before you disturb the bed, and then you can gently remove any soiled or wet bedding. Most bitches prefer to have their pups on the bare wood of the box. Straw or fluffy blankets are not to be recommended, as small fragments are liable to adhere to the wet teats of the bitch and be swallowed by the pups.

It is never advisable to leave more than six to seven pups for the bitch to rear. If she has more than this, it is far better to destroy some if there is no foster mother available. After the first day, it is usually possible to pick some which are less strong than the others, and these are the ones which should be eliminated. By leaving more than six or seven puppies with the mother, you are placing an undue strain on her and eventually all will suffer. It is far better to rear seven healthy, strong puppies and save the stamina of your bitch, than to rear ten or eleven weedy ones.

Feed the bitch entirely on milky foods for the first two days after whelping; she will need a drink every three hours. The milk can be thickened with arrowroot, semolina, etc., and should be well sweetened with glucose or sugar. If all goes well, she can have a meal of finely minced raw meat on the third day, and then be gradually brought back to her normal diet. She will need in addition to her meat, plenty of liquids such as milk, beef tea, etc., and should be fed every three to four hours.

On the fourth or fifth day, the dew claws must be removed from the legs of the puppies. It is a very simple operation if done at this age. With Alsatians it is the custom to remove the dew claws from the hind legs only. Quite often, puppies are born without any, which saves the bother of removing them. It is advisable to have a veterinary surgeon to remove them if you are not an experienced breeder.

After the first week, the nails of the forefeet of the puppies should be snipped every few days to keep them blunt. Great care is necessary not to cut too far down. Only the sharp tips should be taken off with a sharp pair of scissors. If this is neglected, the sharp points of the nails will cause the bitch a lot of unnecessary pain while the pups are suckling, and her teats will become scratched and raw and may well cause her to abandon her duties far too soon.

The eyes of the puppies will open at about fourteen days, and you can then start to supplement the bitch's feeding. Take each puppy in turn, and guide its mouth to the palm of your hand where you have a tiny portion of finely scraped raw beef. Insert a small piece of the meat into the mouth of the puppy and let it get the taste of the meat. Repeat this once or twice, and in no time you will have the puppy taking the meat from the palm of your

LATE I. Ch. anko von Menenmoor of ardwick (Dog), e property of ajor W. Scott.

PLATE II. Ch. Quixotic of Huesca (Dog), the property of Miss S. Kozhevar.

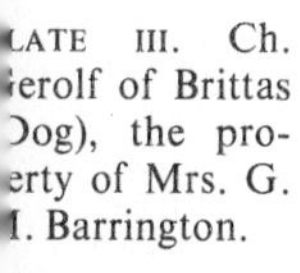

LATE III. Ch. erolf of Brittas Dog), the proerty of Mrs. G. . Barrington.

PLATE IV. Int Ch. Chota of Glandoreen (Bitch), the property of Mr. R. McCullough.

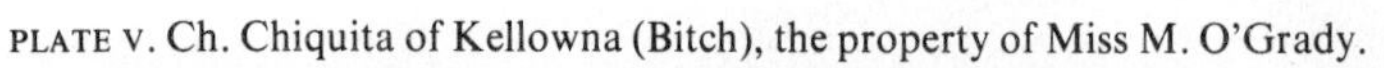

PLATE V. Ch. Chiquita of Kellowna (Bitch), the property of Miss M. O'Grady.

PLATE VI. Ch. Vikkas Donna av. Hvitsand (Bitch), the property of Mr. and Mrs. Elliott.

ATE VII. 'Argus of Rodlyn' as a four-months-old puppy, the property Mrs. R. G. Baker.

PLATE VIII. Litter three weeks old (Puppies), the property of Mrs. Gaywood.

PLATE IX. 'Ajax of Huesca' and 'Diana of Glenrieff' with their young owner in Kenya.

hand without help. Then, when you have them all eating in this way, you can start placing the meat on a saucer instead of your hand, and in a very short time you will have them eating round a dish. One teaspoonful of scraped beef is sufficient for each puppy at a time to start with, but this amount can soon be increased at each meal. Although it takes more time, I advise feeding each puppy individually for the first week or two, so as to be certain that they are getting the right amount. At three weeks puppies can be taught to lap. Place some tepid milky food in a saucer, and encourage the puppy to lap by dipping your finger into it and rubbing it round its mouth. As soon as the puppy tastes the milk, he will go back for more, and will use its tongue to lap. It is best to sweeten the milk with glucose for all young puppies.

From the time you start the supplementary feeding at two to three weeks, you must feed at three-hourly intervals, alternating between scraped raw beef and milk, and you should be able to get in about six feeds per day. During the night, the bitch can be left to feed them. Cow's milk alone is not sufficiently rich in fats to replace the bitch's milk, it is therefore necessary to add cream or powdered full cream milk to bring it up to the required standard. If available, goat's milk is an excellent substitute for the bitch's milk, or the well-known brands of proprietary baby foods are all suitable for puppies.

Having once got the puppies eating meat and lapping milk, the process of weaning is very simple. Gradually increase the amount of food given at each meal, and slowly introduce more solids such as fine cooked oatmeal or breakfast cereal into the milk, and mixing the meat with whole-meal rusk or puppy meal over which you have poured a small quantity of good bone gravy. In this manner, you will have the puppies eating six good meals per day by the time they are six weeks old, and the bitch can be taken away during the day time and only left with them for warmth and feeding during the night. By this time, the bitch's milk will not be of any great value to the pups, so it is best to try to reduce it by giving less food and less liquid to the bitch, and in order that the puppies do not worry her unnecessarily, arrangements should be made so that the bitch can escape from them when she wishes. A high bench on to which the bitch can jump, but which is out of reach of the puppies is a good plan.

At six weeks, all puppies must be dosed for worms, and if this is done successfully at this age, there is no need to repeat the dose for two or three months. Worming is perfectly simple if the instructions given with the medicine are carried out, but here again, it is necessary to watch the motions of each puppy to be certain that the medicine has worked. It is very rare to find a litter without worms, no matter how carefully you may have treated your bitch.

At eight weeks the puppies should be completely independent of the bitch, and ready to go to new homes. It is, in fact, desirable that they should become individuals, and not rely too much on their brothers and sisters. Puppies left too long living as a 'pack' are liable to become nervous and bad feeders when they eventually have to be separated.

CHAPTER 6

THE CARE OF THE STUD DOG

A DOG at stud must be kept in perfect health and condition if he is to produce strong, virile litters with regularity. Good feeding and exercise are most essential, and he will need food containing a high proportion of protein such as meat, fish, eggs, etc., rather than starchy foods which will make him fat and lazy and probably reduce his keenness for stud work. The Alsatian is not fully grown until between two and two-and-a-half years, and it is very undesirable to breed from a dog until fully mature. Stud work at too early an age will not only result in weakly litters, but will arrest the proper growth of the dog himself and cause weakness in the back and hindquarters.

Many breeders like to allow a young dog one test mating (preferably with an older bitch that has already had litters). This can be done when the dog is about eighteen to twenty months, and will prove his fertility.

A healthy, robust dog can be mated two, or even three times per week over a short period, and should then be given a rest. There are usually times of the year when this is possible, as the majority of bitches are mated either in the early spring or early autumn, and in between these periods there are usually times when the dog can be rested and built up.

Always ascertain that the bitch has reached the period of her 'season' when she is likely to stand to the stud dog, before introducing them. Otherwise, the energies of the dog will be used up in his fruitless efforts to mate her before she is ready. He may easily be put off by his failure, and even refuse to try on a subsequent occasion.

If you are sure the bitch is ready, but she still growls or snaps at the dog, it is always advisable to muzzle her or at least to tie a bandage round her mouth to prevent her snapping at the dog until after the mating has been accomplished. She should be kept on a lead and held as still as possible, so as to assist the dog to effect a quick and easy 'tie'.

It is generally considered that the bitch is more certain to get a litter if there is a 'tie' although this is not an absolute necessity, as many litters have been produced without. Any big difference in the height of the two animals to be mated may have to be adjusted by placing them on slightly different levels, or on sloping ground. It is important to keep the bitch as still as possible during the 'tie' or she may injure the dog by any sudden movement on her part. As soon as the mating is finished, take the dog right away to a quiet kennel to rest. Give him a drink of water and if his services are needed again within the next day or so, it is advisable to give him a raw egg beaten up as an extra to his normal diet to build up his stamina.

For normal bitches, one mating is quite sufficient to produce a healthy litter, but if the bitch has 'missed' before, or been an uncertain breeder, it is often desirable to give her a second mating to make more certain. If this is done, it should take place within twenty-four hours of the first mating. It is quite possible for a bitch to conceive from two matings and to whelp separate litters, so this is why the second mating should take place not later than twenty-four hours after the first, or the bitch may have to undergo an over-long and protracted whelping, and suffer great exhaustion. House your stud dog well away from the others, and especially away from bitches at the time they are in season. They will otherwise have a very disturbing influence on the stud dog, causing him to fret and go off his food, and he will wear himself out in his restlessness and efforts to get to them. There is also a big risk that he may injure himself in trying to escape.

The best type of kennel for a stud dog is a brick-built one with metal doors. With all types of wooden kennel there is the danger that he may gnaw his way out, and even though he may not actually escape, he can cause a lot of damage to the kennel, and wear down his teeth.

It is very desirable that all conditions shall have been agreed between the owner of the stud dog and the owner of the bitch *before* the mating takes place, and they should be put down in writing in order to avoid any misunderstanding or differences afterwards. Most regular kennel keepers have stud cards printed. On these they give the particulars of the dog, his pedigree, registration number, etc., and they also state the stud fee, which is normally payable at the time of mating. There is usually a paragraph relating to the care of visiting bitches which are sent unaccompanied. They normally have to be sent at their owner's risk in a box or hamper provided by him, and whilst the stud dog owner undertakes to exercise every care of the bitch during her visit, he does not undertake responsibility. The stud dog owner is entitled to charge for the keep of the bitch during the time he has her at his kennel, and also for the return carriage. The stud fee which has been prepaid is for one mating only unless otherwise stated.

Many stud dog owners are willing to allow a second free mating if the bitch fails to produce a litter, but this is usually on the understanding that notification is given in writing by the tenth week from the date of the mating, and *provided* that the dog is still in their possession. On being notified that the bitch had missed, the stud dog owner could ask for a veterinary surgeon's certificate to that effect, or could inspect the bitch himself should he wish to do so. It is usually understood that if a second free mating is given, it should take place at the bitch's next season.

All these points should be stated quite clearly in writing, as should any arrangement which might be made for the stud dog owner to take a puppy or puppies in lieu of the stud fee. As it is impossible to foretell the sex or number of puppies which will comprise the litter, it is therefore in the interest of both parties to agree as to how the puppies shall be selected. If the stud dog owner agrees to take the pick of the litter instead of the stud fee, that means that he has the first choice of either sex, and if there is one puppy only, that puppy would be his. If on the other hand he had agreed to take two puppies, the first and third pick, and there were only two puppies, he would only be entitled to take one puppy, the first pick, the second would go to the owner of the bitch.

CHAPTER 7

EXHIBITING AND PREPARATION FOR SHOWS

THE show ring is the breeders' shop window and is easily the best way of advertising. The consistent breeding of prize-winning stock is the hall mark of a good kennel, and the demand for stock bearing a well-known kennel prefix is far higher than from one unknown.

Exhibiting in the show ring can be a very interesting hobby if combined with breeding. The satisfaction which comes from winning prizes with dogs which you have bred or reared is a lasting reward for the hard work, patience and expense. But there is a good deal more in it than just having a good dog. That dog must be trained to show off his good points to the judge under conditions very different from his life at home or in the kennel, and there is a great art in handling and in getting the best out of the dog.

Showing is the best way of testing and comparing your stock with others. If you are observant and study the pedigrees of your competitors, you can learn what to expect from popular sires both good and bad.

It is the dogs which win top honours in the show ring that are the most popular sires. Their well-known name will help breeders to sell their puppies, but it does not always follow that an outstanding show dog proves to be a good sire. His progeny in the show ring will soon reveal whether he is prepotent in passing on good or bad points. The same also applies to brood bitches, but to a lesser degree owing to the relatively small number of their offspring compared with those of a popular sire.

If showing is combined with breeding, it means that even when show dogs reach an age when they are no longer in their prime, or have reached a stage when they are unlikely to go very much further in the show ring, they can still prove of value for breeding for quite a number of years. On the other hand, mere showing for showing's sake, can prove a very dead-end pastime. The chance of any animal going right to the top and becoming a champion is fairly remote. The average good dog will have his period of winning, but sooner or later he will become outclassed by younger or better dogs, and unless he can be retired for breeding purposes, the owner is faced with the problem of either giving up showing or replacing the dog with another more promising specimen. It is not easy to find the right sort of homes for Alsatians no longer fit for the show ring, as they are 'one man dogs' and do not take readily to new owners at an adult age.

In a popular breed such as the Alsatian, competition in the show rings is extremely keen, and it is useless to expect to win unless your dog has been conditioned into a state of perfect health, which means correct feeding, exercising, and grooming —none of which can be hurried. The diet must be well balanced, containing a high proportion of protein. Too much starchy or sloppy food will make a dog fat and soft without properly feeding it. There is nothing which replaces good quality raw meat as the main item of the diet, and only the condition of the dog will tell you the quantity that he requires, for dogs, like humans, vary enormously in their requirements.

To look his best in the show ring a dog must be well covered with flesh with no ribs showing, but he must appear muscular and supple. Regular exercise is of the utmost importance and to get an Alsatian into good, hard, show condition, he will need regular daily exercise both on and off the lead. He should have a brisk walk on the lead every day, or he may be taught to trot beside a bicycle ridden in quiet country lanes, but if the latter method is used, great care is necessary to control the speed which enables the dog to trot without breaking into a gallop. In addition to the daily walking or trotting exercise, which for an adult show Alsatian should be at least five miles per day, the dog will also need some freedom to gallop after a stick or ball, or to romp with other dogs in the open air to open up his lungs and extend his muscles. All exercise must be regular and gradual.

In the case of a young dog, or one which has been allowed to get into soft condition, care must be taken at the start not to overdo things. The amount of exercise must be gradually increased day by day, paying special attention to the hardening of the feet before taking the dog for exercise on the hard road, or serious lameness can result. Daily bathing of the feet in salt water will help in the hardening process. I never recommend the exercising of puppies under twelve months beside a bicycle, as it is so easy to overtax their strength. They are best taken for brisk walks on a lead and given plenty of freedom for play.

Daily grooming is also very necessary for the show dog, but fortunately the Alsatian requires no trimming, he is shown as nature fashioned him. All that is needed is a good stiff brush and a comb, with a wash leather or soft cloth for the final polish. Starting at the neck, the coat should be brushed with deep, penetrating movements towards the tail. Take care to remove any loose hair from the brush, with the comb at frequent intervals. This deep penetrating brushing also acts as massage for the muscles, and will be of great help in conditioning the dog. Any matted parts of the hair should be separated with the comb, paying special attention to the fringes and the hair on the underneath of the body. Bathing is not at all necessary; in fact, it is not at all good for the coat, as it takes out the natural oils which protect the dog from wet and cold, and give the glossy appearance. If the dog should get very wet or muddy, the best way of cleaning his coat is to put him for a few hours into a deep bed of clean straw, and he will clean himself. After which, a good brushing will remove any dirt from the coat.

The eyes and ears must also be kept clean. Nothing denotes a healthy condition more quickly than a clear, bright eye. Make sure that the insides of the ears are clean. A few drops of tepid olive oil dropped into the ear, followed by swabbing out with a piece of soft gauze or cotton wool will keep them clean and free from canker. The Alsatian is seldom bothered by canker in the ear owing to the fact that the ears are normally carried erect.

The nails must be kept short, and usually the exercising of the dog on hard surfaces will keep them and feet in condition and the clipping of the nails will not be necessary. If, however, the dog has been kept on grass or soft ground, it may be necessary to clip the nails with special clippers. If this is neglected, it not only looks very unsightly, but will almost certainly affect the dog's movement. I do not recommend a novice to attempt to clip the very tough nails of an adult dog, for it is so easy to cut into the 'quicks' and cause the dog a lot of pain. It is far better to have it done by a veterinary surgeon or an experienced dog trimmer.

Now for the actual presentation of the dog in the ring. To get the best results, daily practice is necessary, going over the whole procedure which will take place in the show ring. Teach the dog to have his teeth examined without a struggle, gently turn back the lips first on one side of the mouth and then the other so that the whole teeth can be seen by a stranger who is taking the place of the judge at home. Put the dog on a long, thin lead, and teach him to take up the right stance, and to remain still on command. Get his weight evenly distributed between his four legs with one hind leg slightly back. Never try to stretch this one hind leg too far back, or you will throw the dog off balance, and he will be forced to lean backwards and so spoil the appearance of his shoulder. Practise this taking up of a natural-looking stance over and over again, using a simple word or command until the dog knows exactly what is expected of him. It is better to stand facing the dog, and encourage him to step towards you by taking backward steps yourself until you have got him into the right position, then raise your free hand and command 'stay'. Reward him with a tit-bit when he obeys. Never relax while the lesson is on, nor allow the attention of the dog to stray from you. You must exert your will power over him, and insist on absolute obedience before you venture into the show ring, for you must remember that he will find all sorts of excitement in the strange surroundings and being amongst other dogs. So your training must be thorough if it is to stand up to this test. He must also be taught to stand still while the judge examines him, he may want to run his hands over the body. The dog which will allow the judge to examine him and look happy about it, is bound to score points over one which shows nervousness or resentment.

Having taught the dog to stand to show off his points, you must next teach him to trot on the lead to show his 'gait'. This is a very important point in judging the Alsatian and is easily one of the most attractive features of the breed. The dog should be taught to trot on a loose lead and to extend his stride to the very utmost without breaking into a gallop. This long reaching gait of the Alsatian is unsurpassed by any other breed. It should be smooth and graceful, with the minimum up and down movement. It has been said that it should be possible to put a glass of water on the dog's back without it being spilled during the slow trot. Really good gait as described above, is only possible if the shoulders and hindquarters have the correct angles in the bone formation, i.e. 'angulation', and must be united by a strong back. Temperament in the show ring also counts for a good deal. The dog which stands firmly for the judge to examine it, and which looks alert and intelligent with his ears pricked is bound to score points. A good deal can be done by training in this respect, but nothing can artificially produce that mystic quality known as 'glamour', which is the hallmark of a beautiful show dog.

The following is the Standard of Points for the breed as approved by the Kennel Cub.

ALSATIAN (GERMAN SHEPHERD DOG)

STANDARD OF POINTS

As approved by The Kennel Club, January, 1950

CHARACTERISTICS.—The characteristic expression of the Alsatian gives the impression of perpetual vigilance, fidelity, liveliness and watchfulness, alert to every sight and sound, with nothing escaping attention; fearless, but with decided suspiciousness of strangers—as opposed to the immediate friendliness of some breeds. The Alsatian possesses highly-developed senses, mentally and temperamentally. He should be strongly individualistic and possess a high standard of intelligence. Three of the most outstanding traits are incorruptibility, discernment and ability to reason.

GENERAL APPEARANCE.—The general appearance of the Alsatian is a well-proportioned dog showing great suppleness of limb, neither massive nor heavy, but at the same time free from any suggestion of weedin-ess. It must not approach the greyhound type. The body is rather long, strongly boned, with plenty of muscle, obviously capable of endurance and speed and of quick and sudden movement. The gait should be supple, smooth and long-reaching, carrying the body along with the

Alsatian during demonstration

Colour photos by Anne Cumbers

Alsatian at work jumping a 6ft fence

Alsatian police dog

Alsatian pup

Playful friends

Alsatians

Police dog giving demonstration

A fine litter of pups

minimum of up-and-down movement, entirely free from stiltiness.

HEAD AND SKULL.—The head is proportionate to the size of the body, long, lean and clean cut, broad at the back of the skull, but without coarseness, tapering to the nose with only a slight stop between the eyes. The skull is slightly domed and the top of the nose should be parallel to the forehead. The cheeks must not be full or in any way prominent and the whole head, when viewed from the top, should be much in the form of a V, well filled in under the eyes. There should be plenty of substance in the foreface, with a good depth from top to bottom. The muzzle is strong and long and, while tapering to the nose, it must not be carried to such an extreme as to give the appearance of being overshot. It must not show any weakness, or be snipy or lippy. The lips must be tight fitting and clean. The nose must be black.

EYES.—The eyes are almond-shaped as nearly as possible matching the surrounding coat but darker rather than lighter in shade and placed to look straight forward. They must not be in any way bulging or prominent, and must show a lively, alert and highly intelligent expression.

EARS.—The ears should be of moderate size, but rather large than small, broad at the base and pointed at the tips, placed rather high on the skull and carried erect—all adding to the alert expression of the dog as a whole. (It should be noted, in case novice breeders may be misled, that in Alsatian puppies the ears often hang until the age of six months and sometimes longer, becoming erect with the replacement of the milk teeth.)

MOUTH.—The teeth should be sound and strong, gripping with a scissorlike action, the lower incisors just behind, but touching the upper.

NECK.—The neck should be strong, fairly long with plenty of muscle, fitting gracefully into the body, joining the head without sharp angles and free from throatiness.

FOREQUARTERS.—The shoulders should slope well back. The ideal being that a line drawn through the centre of the shoulder blade should form a right angle with the humerus when the leg is perpendicular to the ground in stance. Upright shoulders are a major fault. They should show plenty of muscle, which is distinct from, and must not be confused with coarse or loaded bone, which is a fault. The shoulder-bone should be clean. The forelegs should be perfectly straight viewed from the front, but the pasterns should show a slight angle with the forearm when regarded from the side, too great an angle denotes weakness, and while carrying plenty of bone, it should be of good quality. Anything approaching the massive bone of the Newfoundland, for example, being a decided fault.

BODY.—The body is muscular, the back is broadish and straight, strongly boned and well developed. The belly shows a waist without being tucked up. There should be a good depth of brisket or chest, the latter should not be too broad. The sides are flat compared to some breeds, and while the dog must not be barrel ribbed, it must not be so flat as to be actually slabsided. The Alsatian should be quick in movement and speedy, but not like a greyhound in body.

HINDQUARTERS.—The hindquarters should show breadth and strength, the loins being broad and strong, the rump rather long and sloping and the legs, when viewed from behind, must be quite straight, without any tendency to cow-hocks, or bow-hocks, which are both extremely serious faults. The stifles are well turned and the hocks strong and well let down. The ability to turn quickly is a necessary asset to the Alsatian, and this can only be if there is good length of thigh-bone and leg, and by the bending of the hock.

FEET.—The feet should be round, the toes strong, slightly arched and held close together. The pads should be firm, the nails short and strong. Dew-claws are neither a fault nor a virtue, but should be removed from the hind legs at four to five days old, as they are liable to spoil the gait.

TAIL.—When at rest the tail should hang in a slight curve, and reach at least as far as the hock. During movement and excitement it will be raised, but in no circumstances should the tail be carried past a vertical line drawn through the root.

COAT.—The coat is smooth, but it is at the same time a double coat. The under-coat is woolly in texture, thick and close and to it the animal owes its characteristic resistance to cold. The outer-coat is also close, each hair straight, hard, and lying flat, so that it is rain-resisting. Under the body, to behind the legs, the coat is longer and forms near the thigh a mild form of breeching. On the head (including the inside of the ears), to the front of the legs and feet, the hair is short. Along the neck it is longer and thicker, and in Winter approaches a form of ruff. A coat either too long or too short is a fault. As an average, the hairs on the back should be from 1 to 2 inches in length.

COLOURS.—The colour of the Alsatian is in itself not important and has no effect on the character of the dog or on its fitness for work, and should be a secondary consideration for that reason. All white or near white unless possessing black points, are not desirable. The final colour of a young dog can only be ascertained when the outer coat has developed.

WEIGHT and size.—The ideal height (measured to the highest point of the shoulder) is 22-24 inches for bitches and 24-26 inches for dogs. The proportion, of length to height, may vary between 10:9 and 10:8.5.

FAULTS.—A long, narrow, Collie or Borzoi head. A pink or liver-coloured nose. Undershot or overshot mouth. Tail with curl or pronounced hook. The lack of heavy undercoat.

It will be noted that all points in the standard have been designed for utility, for the Alsatian is essentially a working dog, and his structure is free from exaggeration of any kind. Colour is relatively unimportant provided that it is not too pale. Whites or creams are not recognised in the show ring, as it is very seldom that they have the desired black noses and nails.

ENTERING FOR A SHOW

There are certain formalities which have to be carried out before a dog can be exhibited. He must be registered at The Kennel Club in the name of the exhibitor. This means that if the dog was already registered in the name of a previous owner, he must be transferred before he is eligible to be shown. The forms for entry are obtainable from the show secretary, and it is usual for entries to close three or four weeks before the date of the show. The closing date is always stated in the show schedule and on the entry form, and under no circumstances can entries be accepted after this date.

When filling in the entry form it is necessary to state the

registered name of the dog, date of birth, sex, breeder, name of sire and dam and breed. There is also a space provided for the numbers of classes in which the dog is to be entered, and the price if he is for sale. It is also necessary to sign a declaration agreeing to abide by the rules and regulations of The Kennel Club and also that the dog has not suffered from, or been exposed to the risk of distemper or any contagious or infectious disease for the six weeks prior to exhibition, and a further undertaking that they will not be shown if they incur such risk between the date of entry and the day of the show. It is also against The Kennel Club rules to show a dog which has been inoculated with Distemper Virus within fourteen days prior to the show. Failure to carry out all these regulations makes the exhibitor liable to be fined and disqualified by The Kennel Club. If the dog has been exhibited by a previous owner or owners, it is most important to get details of any prizes the dog had won, and more especially the classes in which they have been won in order that you will know for which classes he is still eligible. The definitions of the various classes are given in the show schedule, they are all of a standard definition applicable to all shows of the same category, and are based either on the age of the dog such as Special Puppy (over six and under nine months of age); Puppy (over six and under twelve months of age); Junior (over six and under eighteen months); and Yearling (over six and under twenty-four months). No puppy can be shown under six months of age, and in entering for age classes the dog must be within the age limit stated on the date of the show. Previous wins do not affect entry into age classes.

All other classes are based on previous wins, so it is important to have full details of the dog's show history to avoid entering in a class for which he is ineligible, and so run the risk of disqualification and fine.

The entry fees are charged at so much per class according to the type of the show, and they must be sent with the entry form. At most shows there is also a small charge made for benching when this is provided. All Championship shows (except obedience) must be benched, but it is not compulsory at Open, Limited, or Members' shows.

The prize money is usually offered to the first, second and third winners in each class and is in proportion to the entry fee charged. At Championship shows The Kennel Club offers Challenge Certificates and these are given to the best dog and best bitch of the breed irrespective of the class in which it has been entered. If there are several winners of classes which have not met in competition, they are paraded before the judge and he picks the Challenge Certificate winner from these unbeaten dogs and bitches. It does not automatically go to the winner of the Open class as is so often presumed. A dog or bitch must win three Challenge Certificates under three different judges before he earns the title of 'Champion'.

CHAPTER 8

FAMOUS SIRES AND DAMS WHICH HAVE INFLUENCED THE BREED

It has been pointed out in previous chapters that the Alsatian was little known in Great Britain until after the first World War, but from then until the outbreak of war in 1939 there was a period of approximately twenty years during which the breed became established. Then there came a gap of five to six years during the second World War when practically all breeding of dogs ceased, and this has brought about a dividing line between the pre-war and the post-war dogs. The few shows which were held during the war 1939–46 period were of a small variety, and no dog became a champion during that period, as The Kennel Club withdrew the awarding of Challenge Certificates between 1939 and 1946.

Outstanding amongst the pre-war Sires were:

CHAMPION ALLAHSON OF IF. Owner, Major O. E. Forsyth-Major.

Sire, Allah v.d. Rolandsburg; Dam, Diana of If (v. Humboldpark).
Sire of the following Champions: Ch. Cillahson of Picardy; Ch. Cillas Pinnacle of Picardy; Ch. Danko of Picardy; Ch. Allahson of Kyrle; Ch. Dawn of If; Ch. Jill of Charleville; Ch. Haddon's Allah.

CHAMPION ADALO OF CEARA. Owners, Mrs. and Miss Workman.

Sire Ch. Armin Ernasleib; Dam, Ch. Susi von Boll.
Sire of the following Champions: Ch. Roland of Coulmony; Ch. David of Coulmony; Ch. Donald of Coulmony;

Ch. Atalanta Cothurni; Ch. Farina of Nonington; Ch. Adaletta; Ch. Seffe of Cloverhill; Ch. Odin of Penyghent; Ch. Lutzi of Brittas; Ch. Lothar of Brittas; Ch. Andromeda of Farmcover; Ch. Freia of Ceara; Ch. Danilo of Ingon.

CHAMPION CUNO OF LOUVENCOURT. Owner, Mrs. L. Leonard.

Sire, Ch. Kuno von Brunnenhof; Dam, Ch. Gerta von Simplon.

Sire of the following Champions: ch. Southdown Danko; Ch. Southdown Duskie; Ch. Southdown Dollie; Ch. Alfred of Tulchan; Ch. Saltum Gloria; Ch. Rudolf of Louvencourt.

CHAMPION JANITOR OF PICARDY. Owner, Lt.-Col. J. Y. Baldwin, D.S.O.

Sire, Allei of Picardy; Dam, Beda von Anderton of Picardy.

Sire of the following Champions: Ch. Campanula of Picardy; Ch. Grethel of Quarrymoor.

INT. CHAMPION GEROLF OF BRITTAS. Owner, Mrs. G. M. Barrington.

Sire, Voss von Bern; Dam, Fee (Bell).

Sire of the following Champions: Ch. Ulrica of Brittas; Ch. Yvo of Ravenscar; Ch. Vagabond of Brittas. (Gerolf was just in his prime when the war curtailed all breeding or he would undoubtedly have proved a far greater stud force).

CHAMPION DULO VON MINSWEERT. Owner, Lt.-Col. J. Y. Baldwin, D.S.O.

Sire, Alex von Valkenoord; Dam, Alice v. Minsweert.

Sire of the following Champions: Ch. Aurora of Southavon; Ch. Dante of Charavigne and Quella of Brittas.

CILLA OF PICARDY. Owner, Lt.-Col. J. Y. Baldwin, D.S.O.

Sire, Danko v. Riedeckenburg; Dam, Vera de Terraqueuse.

Dam of the following Champions: Ch. Cillahson of Picardy; Ch. Cillas Pinnacle of Picardy; Ch. Danko of Picardy; Ch.

Grey Shadow; and several other C.C. winners.

CARMEN OF COULMONY. Owner, Miss R. J. Crossman.

Sire, Gunyah of Dysbrook; Dam, Marie Rose.
Dam of the following Champions: Ch. Roland of Coulmony; Ch. David of Coulmony; Ch. Donald of Coulmony; Ch. Merrylass of Coulmony.

CHAMPION SARELLE OF SOHAM. Owner, Mrs. L. Thornton.

Sire, Orto von Simplon; Dam, Sarcee of Soham.
Dam of the following champions: Ch. Southdown Danko; Ch. Southdown Dollie; Ch. Southdown Duskie.

OUTSTANDING POST-WAR SIRES

The post-war period dates from 1946 when Championship shows were reinstated and the breeding of pedigree dogs started again on a large scale. The popular sires at the beginning were not themselves Champions owing to the wartime restrictions, but they were the founders of the new era.

GOTTFRIED OF COULATHORNE. Owner, Mr. A. R. Dyer.
Sire, Ch. Dante of Charavigne; Dam, Caroline of Ranonburg.
Sire of the following Champions: Ch. Neva of Coulathorne (Dam Ingrid of Coulathorne); Ch. Fleur de Lis of Rowley (Dam Irmgarde of Coulathorne); Ch. Honey of Druidswood (Dam Francesca of Druidswood); Ch. Harmony of Druidswood (Dam Francesca of Druidswood); Ch. Alise Tadellos (Dam Delhila Romana).

SOUTHDOWN JEREMY. Owner, Mr. B. C. Dickerson.

Sire, Etzel of Brittas; Dam, Southdown Scilla.
Sire of the following Champions: Ch. Jet of Seale (Dam Helen of Seale); Ch. Southdown Karda (Dam Southdown Queen Bee); Ch. Squire of Rowley (Dam Shene of Rigi); Ch. Jaqueline of Rigi (Dam Silva of Rigi).

MARIO ROMANA. Owner, Mrs. G. Uglione.

Sire, Gottfried of Coulathorne; Dam, Renown of Sálmons.
Sire of the following Champions: Ch. Reginella Romana (Dam Ghita of Ingon U.D. C.D.); Ch. Lyric of Southavon (Dam Isla of Brittas); Ch. Uisgebeata of Brittas (Dam Isla of Brittas); Ch. Carissima of Bolivar (Dam Bolivar Anna of Holtwood).

INGOSOHN OF EROL. Owner, Mr. J. Schwabacher.

Sire, Ingo von Piastendamm; Dam, Franz v.d. Secretainerie.
Sired the following Champions: Ch. Arno of Saba (Dam Empress of Leeda); Ch. Apollo of Saba (Dam Empress of Leeda); Ch. Abbess of Saba (Dam Empress of Leeda).

ETZEL OF BRITTAS. Owner, Mrs. G. M. Barrington.

Sire, Arno v. Bibliserwald; Dam, Ch. Daga of Brittas.
Sired the following Champions: Ch. Fidala of Cranville (Dam Belveda of Cranville); Ch. Daga of Templefields (Dam Quella of Brittas).

INT. CHAMPION VAGABOND OF BRITTAS. Owner, Mrs. G. M. Barrington.

Sire, Int. Ch. Gerolf of Brittas; Dam, Ellengart of Brittas.
Sired the following Champions: Ch. Indigo of Brittas (Dam Katia of Brittas); Ch. Ischka of Brittas (Dam Katia of Brittas); Ch. Rola of Brittas (Dam Vesta of Ivel); Ch. Vikkas Delsa av Hvitsand (Dam Ch. Karaste Karenina av Hvitsand).

CHAMPION ARNO OF SABA. Owner, Mr. M. Scriven.

Sire, Ingosohn of Erol; Dam, Empress of Leeda.
Sired the following Champions: Ch. Poultonoire Artist (Dam Delia of Glendaire); Ch. Altania of Poultonoire (Dam Delia of Glendaire); Ch. Avon Prince of Alumvale (Dam Briarville Crystal of Trystlynn); Ch. Artemis of Iada (Dam Iada Gerta of Celebre); Ch. Hella Secretainerie (Dam Frivolity of Peakhill).

CHAMPION INDIGO OF BRITTAS. Owner, Mrs. J. Beck.

Sire, Int. Ch. Vagabond of Brittas; Dam, Katia of Brittas.

Sired the following champions: Ch. Drakemyre Amber (Dam Magali of Croftholme); Ch. Ansa of Bolivar (Dam Bolivar Anna of Holtwood); Ch. Arlene of Bolivar (Dam Bolivar Anna of Holtwood); Ch. Walgrunde of Brittas (Dam Edrika of Brittas); Ch. Perdita of Kentwood (Dam Nerissa of Kentwood); Ch. Letton Rola of Alsaren (Dam Eroica of Templefields).

CHAMPION DANKO VON MENKENMOOR OF HARDWICK. Owner, Major W. Scott.

Sire, Gd. Ch. Lex Preussenblut; Dam, Ch. Bionda v.d. Buchenhohe, Sch. III.

Sired the following Champions: Ch. Anna Karenina Vitalis (Dam Freda of Oxhey); Ch. Vitalis Amazon (Dam Freda of Oxhey); Ch. Sabre Secretainerie (Dam Frivolity of Peakhill); Ch. Terrie of Glenvoca (Dam Ch. Abbess of Saba); Ch. Cip of Lynrowe (Dam Rampa of Karda); Ch. Southdown Nireus (Dam Ch. Ranee of Karda); Ch. Grizel of Combehill (Dam Sara of Redbyville); Ch. Gitana of Combehill (Dam Sara of Redbyville); Ch. Riot of Rhosincourt (Dam Rhoda of Rhosincourt); Ch. Lodo of Bucklebury (Dam Ilse Secretainerie); Ch. Dora of Eveley (Dam Lady of Littlebrook); Ch. Marquita of Eveley (Dam Walda of Brittas).

CHAMPION AVON PRINCE OF ALUMVALE. Owner, Mr. E. Carver.

Sire, Ch. Arno of Saba; Dam, Briarville Crystal of Trystlynn.

Sired the following Champions: Ch. Invader of Eveley (Dam Walda of Brittas); Ch. Iona of Eveley (Dam Walda of Brittas); Ch. Rebecca of Byenroc (Dam Ilona of Byenroc); Ch. Ransome of Byenroc (Dam Ilona of Byenroc); Ch. Querida of Cranville (Dam Janay of Cranville); Ch. Yokel of Aronbel (Dam Kerry Dancer of Aronbel); Ch. Chiquita of Kellowna (Dam Helium of Kellowna); Ob. Ch. Vaqueel of Kellowna (Dam Helium of Kellowna); Ch. Vikkas Donna av Hvitsand (Dam Ch. Vikkas Delsa av Hvitsand).

These records also show that certain brood bitches have also played an important part as producers of Champions, i.e., SARA OF REDBYVILLE (3), Ch. Grizel and Ch. Gitana of Combehill, also Ch. Edana of Combehill.

BOLIVAR ANNA OF HOLTWOOD (3) Chs. Ansa, Arlene, and Carissima of Bolivar.

ISLA OF BRITTAS (3) Ch. Lyric of Southavon, Ch. Visgebeata of Brittas and Ch. Quince of Southavon.

WALDA OF BRITTAS (3) Ch. Invader of Eveley, Ch. Iona of Eveley. Ch. Marquita of Eveley.

QUELLA OF BRITTAS (2) Ch. Karaste Karenina av. Hvitsand and Ch. Daga of Templefields.

CH. ABBESS OF SABA (2) Ch. Artemis of Glenvoca and Ch. Terrie of Glenvoca.

FREDA OF OXHEY (2) Ch. Anna Karenina Vitalis and Ch. Vitalis Amazon.

FRANCESCA OF DRUIDSWOOD (2) Ch. Honey and Ch. Harmony of Druidswood.

KATIA OF BRITTAS (2) Ch. Indigo and Ch. Ischka of Brittas.

ILONA OF BYENROC (2) Ch. Rebecca and Ch. Ransome of Byenroc.

FRIVOLITY OF PEAKHILL (2) Ch. Hella Secretainerie and Ch. Sabre Secretainerie.

CHAPTER 9

DOGS AND THE LAW

DOG owners have many responsibilities which must be undertaken, and failure to carry them out places the owner in the position of being fined under the law of the country.

Any dog over the age of six months (when it officially ceases to be recognised as a puppy) must have a licence. This licence can be obtained from any Post Office on the payment of 37½p. The licence entitles the person in whose name it is taken out to keep a dog for twelve months beginning on the first day of the month in which it is taken out. It does not apply to any particular dog, but to the owner, who may change the dog he keeps as often as he likes provided that he has a licence for each and every dog he keeps. A licence cannot be handed on to a new owner with the dog as is so often imagined. Even though the original owner no longer keeps a dog, the purchaser must take out a licence in his own name as soon as he accepts the dog. The only exceptions to this rule are for dogs used as guides for blind persons and sheep dogs or herding dogs kept by farmers. Even in these cases, a permit to keep the dog must be obtained, but no fee is charged. There is no such thing as a Breeder's Licence, or Pack licences for packs of hounds or other hunting dogs.

The dog owner is also responsible for seeing that his dog shall wear a collar to which is attached a disc or plate engraved with the name and address of the owner. Large numbers of dogs are lost every year through their owners' neglect in this respect. If every dog which strayed was found to be wearing a collar with the owner's name and address clearly shown, it would save endless work for the Police and the Dogs' Homes, and the owner would also be saved a lot of anxiety. In olden days it was fashionable for valuable dogs to wear very elaborate collars with brass studs and other decorations, partly as a matter of pride on the part of the owner, and also as protection for the dog should he get involved in a fight.

Although the Laws of the Country relating to dogs apply equally to dogs of all breeds, it is obvious that owners of large breeds such as Alsatians have a far greater responsibility to keep their dogs under proper control than the owners of small dogs, because of the added damage they are capable of causing. For instance, a small toy dog might rush out and snap at the heels of tradesmen or passers by, and do no more harm than to make a nuisance of itself, but a large, active dog, such as an Alsatian, which did precisely the same thing might cause serious damage, and be very frightening to people who are not used to them. To merely put a notice on the gate 'Beware of the Dog' does not absolve the owner of responsibility should his dog bite anyone. It is up to him to protect persons coming on to his premises for lawful purposes. Even if the dog is kept chained up, it must not be in a position to reach and injure passers by or those entering the premises for lawful business. On the other hand, a dog can be left loose within the bounds of his master's property by day or night, and should it attack a trespasser who had no right to be there, he would not be held liable for damage thus caused.

It is up to the dog owner to keep the boundaries of his property properly fenced, and even though his neighbour may be the person responsible for keeping the fence in repair, it does not absolve the owner of a savage or destructive dog of the responsibility for damage caused by his dog. He should have erected a fence on his own property in order to keep his dog under control.

It is quite a fallacy to imagine that a dog is entitled to his first bite at a person free. Anyone can take action against the owner of a savage dog without having to prove that the dog had previously bitten someone else, and if he can prove that the owner had previous knowledge that the dog showed a savage disposition towards humans, he would most probably win his case. The law is similar in the case of a dog which attacks other dogs. The owner of an injured dog can summon the owner of the aggressive dog in a Magistrate's Court, and have him ordered to keep the dog under proper control. If, after this, the dog again attacks other dogs or human beings, an order for its destruction can be obtained.

With the heavy volume of motor traffic on the highways, it is desirable for every reason to keep all dogs on leads, not only for their own safety, but for the serious accidents they can cause. It is often said that more road accidents are caused by motorists swerving to avoid loose dogs on the road than from any other cause. It is true that a dog has as much right to be on the highway as motorists, but, like pedestrians, they can only lawfully be on the highway for the purpose of passing and repassing. If they loiter they become trespassers. This law applies whether the dog is accompanied by his master or not. All accidents involving a dog and a motor car or cyclist must be reported in the same way as one between a pedestrian and a vehicle. The matter of responsibility for the accident, and any claims for compensation or damage, resolves itself into a question of the ordinary law of negligence, and the owner of a dog may be found guilty of contributory negligence in not having his dog under proper control. Practically every dog starts life with a natural instinct to chase other animals, especially if the other animal runs away from it. It is up to the dog owner to check this natural desire, and it is never too early to start training a puppy to walk amongst poultry, sheep, and all other farm stock without interfering with them. At the slightest desire shown by the puppy to chase, he should be very swiftly and severely corrected. If this is done often enough while the puppy is young, and the owner's attention is never taken off the puppy so that he is ready to anticipate any lapse with a sharp word of correction, it is usually quite an easy matter to train the puppy to leave other animals alone, including cats and other smaller dogs.

The dog owner is liable in damages for any injury done by his dog to cattle or poultry, and in this case there is no necessity to prove a previous tendency. Cattle includes horses, mules, sheep, goats, and pigs. Although no immediately apparent damage may be done by a dog chasing a ewe in lamb or a milking cow, very serious after-effects can occur. The lamb may be born prematurely and die, or the milking qualities of the cow seriously upset, causing severe loss to the farmer. A large dog such as an Alsatian, if allowed to chase a flock of sheep, can cause many hundreds of pounds worth of damage, apart from a lot of suffering to the sheep.

No one is legally justified in shooting a dog which is merely chasing domestic animals. To be justified in doing this, the dog must be proved to have been in the very act of, and could not in any other way be prevented from, attacking the animal. This is usually a very difficult matter to prove, as the dog has more often than not strayed away from its home or its master and there are no witnesses. Every year large numbers of sheep are killed by untraced dogs, and the farmers cannot be blamed for taking the law into their own hands. On no account should any dog be allowed to stray on its own in the country, especially at night, and the owner should keep it strictly at heel or on a lead when using footpaths, crossing fields or passing through woods. A landlord or farmer is perfectly within his rights in setting wire snares in the open or anywhere else he likes on his land, but spring traps may only be set in holes or tunnels or otherwise covered. The dog owner has therefore no redress if his dog is caught in a snare or trap unless possibly it was set directly on a public footpath where it might equally be a danger to human beings.

Alsatians are often used in continental countries for pulling small carts, but it is an offence in Great Britian for a dog owner to use, or to permit any dog to draw any 'cart, carriage, truck or barrow', or to help to draw one on a public highway. There may be some doubt if the law is, in all cases, limited to a public highway, and if a sledge or toboggan is a carriage of any description, but the intention of the act is clear. It is up to dog owners to see there is no danger of cruelty, even if children are only playing with the dog and a toboggan, or even a soap box on wheels.

The law is strict on matters of cruelty, and persons who are proved guilty of excessive cruelty can be debarred for life from keeping a dog. The owner of a dog may, in fact, be liable at law for permitting the dog to be treated cruelly, together with the person who actually caused the cruelty. The owner of a dog can be liable for cruelty in numerous unsuspected ways, and it must be remembered that *passive* ill treatment is just as much cruelty as is *active* ill treatment. Sending a dog by rail in too small a box, using spiked collars in training, failing to see that a dog received proper treatment during illness, or after an accident, performing, or permitting anyone else to perform, an operation which should be carried out under an anaesthetic by a qualified veterinary surgeon, and doing anything to cause, or failing to do what is necessary to prevent pain and suffering to the animal, are all cases of cruelty to animals.

An act introduced in 1949 makes it illegal for *anyone* except a qualified veterinary surgeon to give treatment of any sort to sick or injured animals. Exceptions are at present made in the cases of certain experienced persons who had given treatment for a number of years prior to the passing of the Act, and who are duly registered as such, but no others will be permitted to so register.

A dog entering Britain from any other country (not including Eire or the Channel Isles) must spend a period of six months in quarantine at one of the specialist isolation kennels which have received Government approval. By this means, we in this country are kept free from the dreaded disease of rabies —extremely dangerous, and known as hydrophobia in humans. The disease is common in most Continental, African, and American countries, and is exceedingly prevalent in most Asiatic and tropical countries. It is easily contracted by other dogs, and by humans from an infected dog, and it is invariably fatal. The necessity of quarantine is proved by the fact that cases of rabies have developed in imported dogs during their period of quarantine in recent years, some of these, in the last month of the period, thus proving the stipulated quarantine is none too long. If a bitch in whelp is brought into quarantine, it is possible, under certain conditions, to remove her puppies after they have been weaned. It is not necessary for the puppies to remain in quarantine for the full period of six months.

CHAPTER 10

OBEDIENCE TRAINING

TRAINING can commence as soon as the puppy is old enough to leave the dam, and this is the ideal age to undertake the proper upbringing and training of an Alsatian. At this early age the puppy has not had time to form any bad habits which have to be broken, nor is it necessary to undo bad training, or worse still, make up for the lack of training which is so often the case in an older dog. Your eight-week-old puppy will be yours for the asking, and you will be able to mould his character and make just what you want of him, especially if you have made sure that you were buying a puppy from an intelligent strain. It will require time and patience, but you will never have cause to regret the time spent during the first few months in teaching your puppy the simple rules of obedience.

Furthermore, your puppy will grow up to be a far happier dog if he is properly disciplined from the start, and he will certainly have far more love and respect for the owner who is firm but just, than for one who allows him to run wild and then has to be harsh with him because he does not obey. Punishment will rarely be necessary if your puppy has grown up from his earliest days to know the difference in the tone of your voice. His sensitive nature will react to your moods, and he will want to please you, and so get that well-deserved praise from you when he has done well. Simple training can become part of his everyday life, he will be automatically obedient if he has never been allowed to do otherwise. There will never come a time when he has to be 'broken' or sent away for a course of Obedience Training under the stern tuition of a professional trainer. This only becomes a necessity for dogs which have been neglected during puppyhood and are suffering from the lack of human contact.

EARLY DISCIPLINE

As part of his early training, I strongly recommend every Alsatian owner to shut his puppy up in a kennel or out-building for an hour or two every day. After he has got over thc initial stage of asking to be let out, he will settle down and rest far more than he would in a house where there are bound to be constant interruptions. The important thing is to never let him out while he is barking or making other efforts to get out. It may mean putting up with a certain amount of noise and inconvenience at the start, but if you are firm, and do not give way, you will find this form of discipline of value for the rest of the dog's life. There are bound to be times when he has to be left alone, and a dog which howls and scratches at doors becomes a nuisance to everyone in the vicinity. It is therefore of the utmost importance to teach your puppy that when he is shut up he must be quiet, and will only be let out if he is so. This is especially important in the case of bitches which will have to be kept shut up during the period of their 'season'.

TEACH THE PUPPY TO 'STAY'

When in the house, the puppy should be given his own comfortable bed or basket and should be encouraged to sleep in it. The easiest way to teach him, is to place him in the bed after he has had exercise and a meal and will be tired and wanting to sleep. Stroke him gently and repeat the command 'Stay' many times. Each time he attempts to get out of the bed put him back again and repeat the command. After a few lessons he will know what you want, and you will gradually be able to command him to 'stay' wherever you wish. Allow him to take his bones and solid rubber balls to his bed, and you will find that he will grow to prefer the comfort of his own bed and you will be able to prevent him jumping up on to your chairs, etc., and covering them with hairs and dirt.

If he is allowed into the dining-room at meal times, insist that he 'stays' in a corner of the room well out of the way, and you will thus prevent him developing the annoying habit of begging at meal times, which can be a nuisance to you and your guests.

SITTING

'Sitting' is another most useful obedience exercise and of great use in a variety of ways. To teach it, you call your puppy towards you and when he is near, and before he has had time to jump up at you, hold a tasty titbit in your one hand out of his reach and gently press on his quarters until he is in a sitting position, repeating sharply and firmly the command 'sit'. You can repeat the same lesson at his meal times by holding the dish up until he has 'sat' for it. Once a dog has learned to sit promptly on command you have achieved a large measure of control over him. For instance, you can teach a puppy not to jump up and smother your best clothes with muddy paw marks by giving a sharp command 'sit' as he comes towards you and seems in danger of jumping up. You can also use it if he is in a mood not to come when he is called. In such circumstances, give him a sharp command 'sit' and then go up to him gently and make a great fuss of him, and so inspire him with confidence, for the chances are, he was afraid to come because he expected you to be angry with him.

Practise the 'sit' exercise at all times, especially when he is out for a walk and running free, always praising him when he obeys and allowing him to run free again afterwards so that he never associates it with any form of punishment.

WALKING TO HEEL

Walking to heel can also be taught while the puppy is very young, and can be taught in combination with the 'sit' exercise. Use a fairly long flexible lead held in your left hand so that it comes in front of your knees, and start by commanding the puppy to 'sit' at your right side facing in the same direction as yourself. Fondle him by rubbing his ears, and at the same time patting your right leg to encourage him to come up close to you. Next, take a few steps forward with a slight jerk of the lead and a sharp command 'heel'. If the puppy hangs back, encourage him to walk forward by patting your right leg to bring him up level with you. As soon as you have got him walking beside you on a loose lead, practise stopping by bringing your heels together with a click and repeating the command 'sit'. After each 'sit' at heel, fondle him with your right hand and encourage him to sit squarely by your side. Giving the lead a sharp jerk move forward again with the command 'heel', gradually introducing right and left turns, and finally about turns with intermittent 'sits'.

Having perfected this walking to heel on the lead, you next detach the lead, if possible without the puppy realising, and you then go through the same commands and movements with the puppy free. The moment his attention wanders, or he gets too far away from you, put him back on the lead and practise again with a few gentle but sharp jerks of the lead.

Heel work can best be taught in a narrow passage way or cul-de-sac, as there is less opportunity for the dog to wander far away from you, and you can more easily command his full attention.

RETRIEVING

Most puppies enjoy carrying a soft article in their mouths, and one can therefore divert this natural instinct into teaching the 'retrieve' which is a most useful exercise, and can be used in a variety of ways later on.

First teach the puppy to carry an easily held article such as a rolled-up leather glove or a similar article made into a shape which is easy for the dog to carry, and later on to pick up from the ground. Some dogs are so keen to carry that you can start straight away to throw the article a few yards away and give the command 'fetch' or 'carry' and then encourage them to return to you with the article held in their mouth. Others are best taught to first hold the article and to give it up willingly on the command 'drop'. When teaching this exercise, always try to have your hands ready to take the article by holding them on each side of the dog's mouth, and so avoid letting the article drop to the ground when the dog releases his hold.

When you have once taught the dog that 'carry' means holding the article in his mouth, and 'drop' means placing it in your outstretched hands, you are well on the way in teaching the 'retrieve'. One word of warning—never let the dog play with the article which you use for the retrieve exercise, and never confuse the serious work of retrieving with running after sticks or balls.

Let his play and playthings be things apart, and never use the words of command unless you are prepared to see that they are properly carried out.

It is a curious thing that some dogs will learn to retrieve in a few lessons, but in other cases it is the exercise which presents the greatest difficulties. It seems as though the dog just cannot understand what is wanted, and then suddenly one day you will find your patience has been rewarded and from that moment, all is plain sailing. Retrieving can only be taught by patience, kindness, and perseverance. Never lose your temper, or try to hurry things, no matter how obstinate the dog may seem, or you will destroy his confidence in you. If you have difficulty in getting the dog to take the article from your hand, gently open his jaws by inserting your fingers into the sides of his mouth, and quickly, but gently, place the article into his opened mouth. Then close his jaws round the article and hold them together with your two hands, repeating many times the word 'carry'. After a few seconds, release your hold and command 'drop', having your hands placed ready to take the article. In all the preliminary retrieve practice, stand facing the dog, as you are better able to hold his attention if you can look into his eyes.

When you are sure that the dog will take the article from your hand and hold it in his mouth until commanded to 'drop', next hold the article a few inches below his mouth so that he has to reach forwards and downwards to take it. Gradually increase this distance until you have finally reached the ground. The moment you can place the article on the ground, take your hand away, and command 'carry' with the certainty that the dog will pick up the article and deliver it to hand, the main difficulties are over, for he has now learned to carry, to pick up, and to deliver to hand.

It is now just a matter of daily practice, increasing distance step by step by placing the article farther and farther away. You next command the dog to sit at heel whilst you throw the article a few yards away, and by repeating the command 'sit' many times you will be able to prevent him running forwards until you give the final command 'fetch' or 'carry'. Always insist that he brings the article right up to hand and sits for you to take it from him.

Having practised retrieving on level ground where the article is clearly visible to the dog when thrown, you now do the same thing on uneven ground or in longish grass, so that although the dog still sees you throw the article, he cannot see exactly where it drops. He will go forward on the command to 'fetch' or 'carry' and find that he can no longer see the article, so he will now automatically use his nose to find the article by scent. You will thus have reached the momentous stage when you have taught your dog to use his nose and not his eyes to find hidden articles carrying your own scent.

As soon as this has been perfected, you can next begin to vary the type of article you use. A dog which has been properly taught to retrieve will bring back anything he is capable of carrying, including metal articles, and can be of real use to his owner in finding articles lost in long grass and places not easily accessible.

Having first taught your dog to follow your own scent, you can then enlist the help of a friend to teach the dog to work on a different scent. The friend must hold his hand over the dog's nose for long enough to enable the dog to get his scent, and you then send the dog to retrieve an article carrying the friend's scent, which of course, has not been handled by you.

SCENT DISCRIMINATION

This exercise is merely a retrieve, but the dog must be taught to select from a number of articles placed near to each other, the one which carries the scent which he has been given. In police work, this has often been the means of identifying criminals who may have left some tell-tale article behind at the scene of their crime. The police dog is given the scent from the article and from it has been able to track and identify the owner.

THE DOWN OR DROP EXERCISE

As in all other exercises, the 'down' must first be taught on a long lead. With the lead held firmly in the left hand, place your foot over the lead so that it runs freely under your instep. Give a sharp word of command 'down' and simultaneously pull the lead with the left hand so that the dog is forced down to the ground with his forelegs extended into a lying position. At the same time raise your right hand above your shoulder extended straight upwards in a kind of Nazi salute. This exercise can be taught in other ways, but I have found this is the most effective. The element of surprise which the dog feels when he finds himself being pulled to the ground by the lead under your shoe, need not be made alarming to him, especially if you give plenty of praise the moment he is on the ground. You will find he will soon learn to drop on command without any pulling of the lead. The upraised right arm used in conjunction with the word of command is valuable because there may be a time when you want to drop your dog from a distance, or under such circumstances when he would be unable to hear your voice, and will obey on the sign alone. The 'down' exercise can be used when you wish to leave your dog in one place and know that he will still be there when you come back, this is usually a combined word of command 'Down'—'Stay' given in firm slow tones.

Then there is the distant control value of the exercise. For instance, you may wish to halt your dog for some reason when he is coming towards you. There may be danger of some sort such as an oncoming car. By commanding your dog to 'down', an accident may be avoided. In these circumstances the command must be given very sharply and combined with the upraised arm movement. The same also applies should you wish to prevent your dog from running away.

The foregoing notes on training are not intended to be full instructions on how to train a dog to competition standard, they are merely hints on how the pet dog owner can train his dog to be well behaved, under control, and a pleasure to own.

The following general hints on training should be remembered.

Never commence any training during the initial stages unless you have sufficient time at your disposal to complete the lesson, for you must always be able to finish up on a note of praise.

Never undertake training if you yourself are out of sorts or your nerves on edge, for you will undoubtedly transmit this to your dog, and make work more difficult.

Always remember that dogs are not machines. They have their good and bad days, and if you feel that it is a bad day on which you are making little progress, go back to something quite simple which you know the dog can do, praise him, and finish for the time being. The chances are that tomorrow things will be quite different.

Always use words of command which are short and easy for the dog to understand. Rely on the tone of your voice to convey to the dog whether he is right or wrong. Encourage him when he looks like doing the right thing, and be lavish with your praise when he does well. A sharp word of correction is usually sufficient, but never nag, for remember that the dog cannot answer back.

Always train your dog in the early stages in a quiet spot, well away from noise and other disturbances, and especially from other dogs. He can be taught to work in the company of other dogs, and in strange places when he has learned what he has to do, but you will make far better progress in the initial stages if you can command his full and undivided attention.

Never be tempted to show off your dog's cleverness before your friends, until you are sure that he will be able to carry out your commands. It is humiliating both for you and the dog if he has to be corrected before others.

Always treat training as a lesson, and having come to the end of the lesson, let your dog off the lead for a good romp and a game, this happy ending will become associated in his mind, and he will come out for the next lesson, keen and anxious to please.

Never lose patience with your dog, no matter how obstinate or stupid he may seem. If you have difficulty with him, go right back to the beginning, and behave as though he was having his first lesson, going slowly through each stage until you arrive at the point where he failed. You may find that the repetition of the early training will refresh his memory and inspire him with confidence. If this is the case, praise him profusely and stop training for the day. If, on the other hand, he still falters at the same point, go back to something quite simple which you know he can do, praise him, and call it a day.

For those who may be interested in competitive Obedience Tests, the following is a list of the exercises to be carried out at all shows held under The Kennel Club Rules.

ANY VARIETY OBEDIENCE

DEFINITION OF CLASSES

No bitch in season allowed to compete in Obedience Test.

Dogs entered in Obedience Classes must be registered at The Kennel Club and entered in the Obedience Record.

In all tests the handler may use the dog's name with a command or signal without penalty.

In all the following Definitions of Tests 1st prize wins at Limited and Sanction Show Obedience Tests will not count when entering for Open and Championship Obedience Tests.

In Novice, Test A and Test B, handlers may use their own dumb-bells.

In composite exercises and the Sit and Down the points will be graduated.

All exercises must include a FINISH.

SPECIAL BEGINNERS

For handlers and dogs that have not won a First Prize in an Obedience Test or Championship Working Trials.

Handlers will not be penalised for encouragement or extra commands except in the Sit and Down. In these Tests at the discretion of the judge, handlers may face their dogs.

1—HEEL ON LEAD, 15 points; 2—HEEL FREE, 20 points; 3—SIT ONE MINUTE, handler in sight, 10 points; 4—DOWN MINUTES, handler in sight, 20 points; 5—RECALL FROM SIT OR DOWN, position at handler's choice. Dog to be recalled by handler when stationary, sit in front, go to heel —all on command of judge to handler. Distance at discretion of judge. Exercise commences when handler leaves dog on judge's command, 10 points; 6—RETRIEVE ANY ARTICLE provided by handler, 25 points. Total 100 points.

NOVICE

For dogs that have not won a First Prize in an Obedience Test (Special Beginners excepted) or Championship Working Trials.

Handlers will not be penalised for encouragement or extra commands except in the Sit and Down. In these Tests, at the discretion of the judge, handlers may face their dogs.

Exercises and points in Nos. 1 to 5 same as Special Beginners. 6—RETRIEVE A DUMB-BELL, 25 points. Total 100 points.

TEST 'A'—UNDERGRADUATE

For dogs that have not won four 1st prizes in Obedience Tests (Special Beginners and Novice excepted) or Championship Working Trials.

Simultaneous command and signal will be permitted. Extra commands or signals will be penalised.

1—HEEL ON LEAD, 20 points; 2—HEEL FREE, 20 points; 3—SIT ONE MINUTE, handler in sight, 10 points; 4—RECALL FROM SIT OR DOWN, position at handler's choice. Dog to be recalled to heel by handler, on command of judge, whilst handler is walking away, both to continue forward. Exercise commences when handler leaves dog on judge's command, 10 points; 5—RETRIEVE A DUMB-BELL, 25 points; 6—DOWN FIVE MINUTES, handler out of sight, 30 points; 7—SCENT DISCRIMINATION, handler's scent on handler's article. Unsuitable articles may be rejected at the discretion of the judge, 30 points. Total 145 points.

TEST 'B'—GRADUATE

Obedience Champions are not eligible for Test 'B'.

At Members' Shows.—For dogs that have not won four 1st prizes in Test 'B' Graduate, Test 'C' Open, or Championship Working Trials.

At Open and Championship Shows.—For dogs that have not won four 1st prizes in Obedience Tests or Championship Working Trials. Wins in Special Beginners, Novice, Test 'A' and any Test at Members' Shows excepted.

One command, by word or signal, except in Exercise 4. Extra commands or signals will be penalised.

1—HEEL ON LEAD, 20 points; 2—HEEL FREE, 20 points; 3—SIT TWO MINUTES, handler out of sight, 20 points; 4—SEND AWAY, DROP, and RECALL. On command of judge to handler, dog to be sent away in direction indicated by judge. After the dog has been dropped handler will call the dog to heel whilst walking where directed by judge and both will continue forward. No obstacle to be placed in path of dog. Simultaneous command and signal permitted in send away but as soon as the dog leaves the handler, the arm must be dropped, 40 points; 5—RETRIEVE A DUMB-BELL, 25 points; 6—STAND ONE MINUTE, handler at least ten paces away, 10 points; 7—DOWN TEN MINUTES, handler out of sight, 50 points; 8—SCENT DISCRIMINATION, handler's scent on article provided by judge. A separate similar article to be used for each dog. This exercise to follow the DOWN. Article to be given to the handler as he leaves the ring for the DOWN. No points will be awarded if the article is given to the dog, 40 points. Total 225 points.

TEST 'C' OPEN

One command, by word or signal, except in exercise 3. Extra commands or signals will be penalised.

1—HEEL FREE, including fast and slow. Figure 8 may be included at judge's discretion, 40 points; 2—SIT TWO MINUTES, handler out of sight, 20 points; 3—SEND AWAY, DROP, and RECALL, as in Test 'B', 40 points; 4—RETRIEVE ANY ONE ARTICLE which must not be in any manner injurious to the dog (definitely excluding food or glass). The article to be picked up easily by any breed of dog and clearly visible to the dog. A separate similar article to be used for each dog, 30 points; 5—DOWN TEN MINUTES, handler out of sight, 50 points; 6—SCENT DISCRIMINATION, judge's scent on piece of material not less than 6 inches by 6 inches provided by judge. A separate similar piece to be used for each dog. Method of taking scent at handler's choice, 50 points; 7—DISTANT CONTROL. Dog to sit, stand, and down, in one place not less than ten paces from handler, in any order on command from judge to handler. Six instructions to be given in the same order for each dog. Excessive movement in any direction by the dog, having regard to its size, will be penalised, 50 points; 8—ADVANCED STAND, SIT, and DOWN. Handler to walk with dog at heel free, leave dog standing (sitting or down) when judge commands and continue forward alone without hesitation round the ring until he reaches dog, both then continue forward, when other positions will follow in a similar manner. Order of positions (same for each dog) at judge's discretion, 40 points. Total 320 points.

ADDITIONAL EXERCISE.—Which may be included at open-air shows where conditions are satisfactory: 9—SEEK BACK (dog to seek flat inconspicuous article, minimum ten paces. Dog must walk at heel, walk will include left and right turns. Time limit, 5 minutes), 40 points.

The Kennel Club will offer an Obedience Certificate Dog and an Obedience Certificate Bitch for winners of 1st prizes in Test 'C' Dog and Test 'C' Bitch at a Championship Show, provided that the exhibits do not lose more than 10 points out of 320, and provided also that the Tests are open to all breeds.

Judges must also award a Reserve Best of Sex provided that the exhibits have not lost more than 10 points out of 320.

CHAPTER 11

AILMENTS

It is an astounding fact that a large proportion of pet dog owners take a delight in dosing and doctoring dogs at the least excuse, and many unfortunate dogs are constantly being drenched with patent medicines or 'condition powders'. Luckily most of the latter are harmless, but many of them are entirely useless.

An ordinary healthy dog, properly fed and looked after on the principles explained in the foregoing chapters, requires neither condition powders nor medicine, and is much better if left to live a normal life.

In the event of an unfortunate accident or illness, professional advice should immediately be sought, and treatment of nothing except the simplest of minor ailments should be attempted by the layman. Legislation has now been put into action which makes it illegal for a person not properly qualified to give treatment to animals. This is not at all out of place as it is regrettable that many of the 'Pet Stores' to be found in towns gave diagnosis, treatment and prescriptions for animals which were usually incorrect and in many cases dangerous.

No one except a graduate at one of our big Veterinary Colleges can use the letters M.R.C.V.S. (or F.R.C.V.S.) after their name and, naturally, a dog is perfectly safe in the hands of anyone having this qualification. If the fees charged by a qualified veterinary surgeon cannot be afforded by a dog owner, free advice and treatment can be obtained at the clinics run by the various charitable organizations, such as those of the Royal Society for Prevention of Cruelty to Animals and the People's Dispensary for Sick Animals.

Having received advice from a properly qualified person, it should be acted upon with the same care and conscientiousness that one would observe in carrying out a doctor's instructions regarding a sick child. The directions regarding dosages, etc., are most important and must be followed exactly. This is as important for dogs as it is for humans. The proprietary dog medicines put on the market by reputable firms of veterinary chemists are excellent if used with common sense. The directions given on the bottle must be rigidly adhered to; the correct dose is always stated on the labels of proprietary medicines and on veterinary surgeons' prescriptions.

The doses of a medicine for dogs are calculated in relation to the weight of full-grown dogs of the particular breeds. When the dose is stated to be 'from so much to so much', the smaller dose is that suitable for a full-grown dog of 15 lbs. in weight, and the larger for one of 45 lbs. or over; doses for dogs of other weights must be calculated proportionately. For a puppy aged six weeks to three months, a quarter of a dose should be given, and half a dose for one three to six months old; the full dose being for a full-grown dog of the breed.

On no account should human medicines be administered, as it is most unsafe to assume that these are equally suitable for dogs. For instance, it would be quite safe for a man to take a dose of Calomel which would be sufficient to kill two large dogs. Common salt in small quantities is a strong emetic for dogs and is poisonous to them in any quantity.

The first sign that a dog is 'off-colour' is usually that he does not finish up his feed with his usual gusto, or that he refuses it altogether. This, in itself, is not serious as a dog can quite easily fast for forty-eight hours without ill-effects, but it should be regarded as a warning and other signs of ill-health, such as the dog becoming unnaturally listless; the nose being hot and dry; the eyes lacking their usual brightness, or discharge from the eyes or nostrils, must be watched for.

Most illnesses start in the stomach and are invariably the result of incorrect feeding or of insufficient exercise. A milk aperient of a dose of Epsom salts (one teaspoonful to four teaspoonfuls) is always a safe preliminary treatment in any illness, and if the trouble has been definitely traced to the stomach a stronger aperient of Castor oil (two teaspoonfuls to two tablespoonfuls) may be given. Professional advice should be sought if the dog is not better in forty-eight hours or, of course, if there is any sign of the dog becoming worse in the meantime.

SKIN TROUBLES are usually the result of digestive trouble, brought on by wrong feeding, dirty food bowls, or by lack of exercise. Skin trouble will make itself evident by the dog showing there is irritation of the skin by scratching or rubbing himself, and by the appearance of red patches or pustules on the skin which will, in due course, discharge. The dog must first be cleansed internally; the cause of the digestive trouble removed, and a good oil skin dressing obtained and applied as directed.

BLEEDING from an external wound, if not excessive, should be arrested by the application of alternate compresses of cotton wool soaked in hot and cold water. If the bleeding is from a vein the flow will be continuous and the blood will be dark in colour; this should be easily arrested by the application of compresses.

If the bleeding is from an artery the blood will be bright red and will spurt in unison with the heart beats. If this is observed a tourniquet should be tied round the limb between the wound and the heart and professional assistance should immediately be called.

In all cases of internal bleeding, evident from the discharge of blood from the mouth or rectum, the dog should be kept quiet and still and a veterinary surgeon sent for at once.

Many puppies suffer from CAR SICKNESS when taken out in a car the first time or two, but they usually grow out of it. In some cases the disease becomes chronic and there seems to be no permanent cure in these cases. A dog should not be fed for at least two hours before starting a car journey and if the dog has a tendency to car sickness it is better to extend this period up to six hours. The dog should be made to lie down quietly in the car and should be placed where there is the minimum amount of swaying motion.

CHOKING: A piece of bone or hard gristle too large to pass down the gullet may get lodged in a dog's throat. This can usually be removed with the fingers, or turned so that it can be pushed down into the stomach. Alternatively the object can sometimes be moved by persuading the dog to swallow a few pieces of meat. If the object cannot be easily moved by these methods a vet. must be immediately called in.

CONSTIPATION is usually the result of incorrect feeding which has weakened the digestive juices, or it may be through insufficient exercise. An aperient, such as Castor oil, will usually remove the cause, and steps should be taken to avoid its recurrence.

COUGH, OR HUST: It is not easy for the inexperienced to distinguish between the various coughing sounds made by the dog and unless the dog reacts to a simple canine cough cure within forty-eight hours it is better to seek professional advice. Even a simple cough neglected, may result in serious complications, but a cough is usually a symptom of some other disease and the real cause must be sought.

Superficial CUTS and WOUNDS are best left alone for nature and the dog's tongue to effect a cure, but if the wound is in such a position as to be inaccessible to the tongue a dab of Iodine, Friar's Balsam or of T.C.P. should be applied and this is usually sufficient. Stitching of wounds is seldom successful owing to the impossibility of keeping the dog still afterwards, and to the danger of the dog tearing or biting the stitches out. It should on no account be attempted by the layman.

DIARRHOEA is invariably caused by wrong feeding, dirty dishes and using up stale food which has been left over from a previous meal, or feeding tainted food. A mild purge of Castor oil should be given and the faults in the diet immediately rectified.

It is an old-fashioned idea that DISTEMPER is bound to attack every dog at some time or other, but actually nothing is farther from the truth. Very nearly 100 per cent. immunity is now obtained by inoculation of the dog by a qualified veterinary surgeon and it must be remembered that the proper serum can only be obtained and administered by a qualified vet. Even if the dog does contract distemper after it has been inoculated, the attack is invariably slight and responds to proper nursing.

The disease takes many forms and has many different symptoms, and the term is, in fact, used for any illness which carries symptoms which are typical: actually little is, as yet, known about several diseases which are grouped together as 'distemper'. If a dog shows any signs of fever, husky cough, serious loss of appetite, or rapid loss of condition, especially if these are accompanied by shivering fits, vomiting and/or diarrhoea, and discharge from the nose and eyes, it should be immediately isolated from other dogs, kept warm and quiet and a veterinary surgeon consulted. The vet's instructions should be carried out implicitly, as the cure of distemper and the prevention of serious secondary complications are entirely a matter of good nursing; in a similar manner to the treatment of 'flu in humans.

The EYE is a delicate organ and no attempt should be made by amateurs to treat any serious diseases or injuries to the eye. Slight discharge from the eyes may be caused by slight cold or from a draught. This should be wiped off with swabs of cotton wool, one swab once across the eye only, and the eye bathed with swabs dipped in lukewarm Boracic acid solution. If the discharge does not clear up from this treatment it is a symptom of a more serious complaint and professional advice must be obtained.

Grass seeds, or such small foreign bodies, are often the cause of an eye becoming inflamed and swollen; these must be searched for and removed and the eye bathed with Boracic acid lotion.

If acid or such corrosive liquid or powder gets into a dog's eye a purse should be made of the eyelids and Castor oil or Glycerine should be poured in.

On no account should dogs, when being taken out in a car, be allowed to hang their heads out of an open window. A large number of eye-colds, with serious consequences in many cases, are caused through this.

The condition of the dog's FEET should be noted daily. If a reasonable amount of exercise is taken on hard roads this should keep the pads and claws in good condition, but if this is not the case the pads may become too hard and cracked, or too soft and sore, and the nails too long.

If the nails appear to be excessively long, the dog should be taken to a Clinic to have them cut; this is a simple operation, but should on no account be attempted by anyone who has not been taught the operation, or who does not possess the proper instrument. Especial care must be taken regarding the 'Dew Claws' as these, having no bearing on the ground, grow rapidly and are liable to grow right round and pierce the leg.

The pads of the feet should receive constant attention. Any thorns or flints picked up at exercise being removed and the wounds treated with Iodine. If the pads are too soft and inclined to be sore through insufficient exercise, especially if it is always on soft ground, they should be bathed daily in a solution of alum and water. If the pads become too hard and cracked a dressing of crude Lanoline should be applied daily.

Tar from the roads, drying on the pads, is a frequent cause of irritation and soreness, and the feet should be examined carefully for this if the dog has been near a soft tarred road. Any tar on the pads should be removed with ether in preference to turpentine or paraffin; nail polish remover can be used in an emergency.

FITS AND HYSTERIA have numerous causes and are invariably the symptoms of a disease. In the case of a dog being suddenly taken in a fit, he should be immediately covered with a coat or rug and placed in a dark, cool room, until he has worked himself out of it. On no account must any attempt be made to give treatment or medicine while the fit is on, but when the dog is well over it, a dose of Potassium Bromide (7 grains to 20 grains) or Aspirin (5 grains to 15 grains), both in water, may be given.

The cause of the fits must be ascertained and for this professional advice must be taken. Worms or stomach trouble, distemper, teething in puppies and, sometimes, mites in the ears are common causes of fits, and the so-called Canine Hysteria is still somewhat of a mystery to veterinary science. Wrong feeding is by far the most common cause of fits and the diet should be completely changed after a dog has suffered from them. The hard, indigestible biscuit meals, manufactured by unknown firms, are frequently found to be the cause of fits.

It is next to impossible to prevent FLEAS ever appearing on a dog, as they can be picked up by the dog from grass, but their presence in any quantity is entirely caused by neglect. Extermination of rats and frequent thorough cleaning of the kennel, bedding, bench, grooming kit, coats and anything belonging to the dog is the best preventative, and together with the removal and drowning in paraffin of any fleas found on the dog during the daily grooming, will keep the dog free from these parasites.

It is exceedingly fortunate that in our island country we are free from the dreadful disease RABIES; for this blessing we should be grateful to the stringent quarantine laws enforced. The period of six months quarantine which is required is none too long, as cases have appeared in imported dogs even after this time. Anyone who has lived in a rabies infected country will agree that the freedom we have in this matter is one of our greatest blessings, and any attempt to avoid the quarantine regulation should be made a criminal offence.

WORMS are a frequent source of canine ailments and several species are liable to attack the dog. It is impossible to prevent the eggs entering the dog's stomach, where they eventually hatch and the worms attach themselves to the lining of the intestines; here they draw nourishment from, and live at the expense of, their host.

Rapid loss of condition, distended stomach and dullness of eyes and coat are signs of the presence of worms in a dog; when present in large quantities, worms or segments of them, may be passed in the dog's motions, and dogs will frequently rub their anus along the ground owing to the irritation caused by worms.

Roundworms and Tapeworms are the two varieties most frequently found in dogs, and when it has been ascertained which variety is infecting the dog, a good proprietary worm powder should be given, care being taken that the dose is suitable to the size of the dog and for the type of worm present. The directions regarding fasting the dog before administering the medicine must be strictly obeyed.

CHAPTER 12

NOTES ON JUDGING

It should be the aim of every judge when he undertakes a judging engagement, to find dogs for his prizewinners which are as near to the breed standard as possible. The Standard of Points has been drawn up to describe the ideal, and fortunately those points are all based on usefulness, and are not merely fads or fancies.

Whilst it is obvious that allowances must be made for a certain amount of variation in the manner in which individual judges interpret that standard, they should be agreed regarding the main essentials. It is the slight difference of opinion which keeps dog shows going, it would be a dull procedure if the same dog always won, and I suppose the perfect specimen is yet to be seen.

Every judge has his own pet likes and dislikes, and when applied to his own kennel he can indulge in these preferences to his heart's content, but he should take great care not to allow this to influence his judging in the show ring.

Colour often plays far too important a part. Certain judges are known to only care for black and tans, and others for greys or sables, but it must be borne in mind that the standard allows for a very wide variety of colours, and is, in any case, a very minor point compared with structural requirements, so one should always take care not to overlook a really good dog because his colour does not catch the eye. Nobody can deny that a really beautifully marked dog with rich colouring will always demand further inspection, and there is an old saying amongst horse breeders that 'a good horse is never a bad colour' and I think that this also applies to dogs.

The *only* way to judge successfully and consistently is to regard the dog as a *whole*. Sum him up in your eye both standing and moving, and then decide where *on balance* he is better or worse than his competitors. Comparison is the safest way, for seen alone, a dog may appear to be first class, but the acid test is to see him against others.

During my many years of judging, I have so often been disappointed when I have discovered what appeared to be a real 'star' entered in the lower classes. Compared with the other Maiden or Novice entrants he has shone above all his competitors, and at first sight it seems that here is a real 'discovery' that is going to make a strong bid when it comes to judging for the Challenge Certificate. He is eventually brought out to challenge, and must then meet all the unbeaten dogs. In cases of this kind, I always try to see him against the whole of my Open class, for here he will have to stand comparison with mature and experienced dogs and handlers, and whereas in the Maiden or Novice class he made all his competitors appear mediocre, he himself may now appear so.

In a slow maturing breed like Alsatians, I never seriously consider puppies or Juniors for the highest honours, for one knows how often a puppy will change with maturity, especially if he looks too perfect as a youngster.

A good judge will *never* overlook a serious unsoundness, no matter how lovely the dog may be in other respects, for it must be borne in mind, that unsoundness is a malformation of some kind (unless the result of an accident) and is likely as not to be transmitted. It is therefore damaging to a breed to award a prize to an unsound dog, for it is the prizewinners which get used for breeding, especially the males. A sound dog of good average points is of far greater value to the breed than one with superb qualities coupled with an unsoundness which may take generations to breed out.

I do not consider that one can judge 'temperament' in the show ring beyond weeding out the obviously shy or savage ones. Provided that a dog will stand quietly for me to examine him, and will show off his paces and look happy about the proceedings, I think that is all one can expect. Temperament tests can be both useless and misleading according to the manner in which they are applied and I think they are best left out. I disapprove of the practice of some Continental judges who flap catalogues or brandish sticks in the ring as a test for temperament. It is far easier to teach a highly strung and nervous dog to put up a show of 'attacking', than the placid, even-tempered one who would be one's real defender in case of need. A lot can be learned about temperament by studying the expression of the eye, and the use which an Alsatian makes of his ears.

'Good gait' after all, is only the proof of good conformation. Without such essentials as good shoulder formation, well angulated quarters, and a strong back, good gait is impossible, and it is only the imcompetent judge who looks for it in a dog of faulty conformation. It is seldom that judging rings are big enough to judge gait except at a slow trot, but many great experts say that this is the natural gait of a sheepdog, and it is certainly just as easy to pick out those with the smooth, effortless gait, with all the component parts working in unison, at a slow trot as at speed, the latter merely looks a little more spectacular, and exhausts the handlers quicker. I always remember the advice of the great von Stephanitz who said 'Beware of the dog with the too crouching gait, and remember that fear lends wings.'

Good condition must be taken into consideration, for not only does it add to the outward appearance, but it denotes a healthy state. A well-exercised dog will show it in the strength and suppleness of his muscles and in the condition of his feet. A clean, shining coat will also show health and care on the part of the owner. Judges can do much to keep a breed on an even keel by never going for extremes, and by noting any tendencies towards a common fault which may be creeping into the breed, and by giving a timely word of warning. One word of advice for the novice judge. *Never* try to judge on points.

In the early days a breed standard was published very much as it is today, but against each point was allowed so many marks out of the total, the idea being to show the relative importance of each point.

On a few occasions I have seen judges try to judge by an elaborate system of book-keeping. They studied each dog in turn and allotted marks for each point as mentioned in the standard, according to how near they considered he approximated to the ideal. Then, having been through all the points with each dog, they then totalled up the marks. I can only say that the results were ludicrous. It is only by regarding the dog as a whole, and by having a natural 'Eye' that one can ever satisfy either oneself or the exhibitor.

TEN GOOD REASONS WHY THE ALSATIAN IS USED ALMOST EXCLUSIVELY FOR WAR WORK AND POLICE WORK

1. The Alsatian learns and thinks quickly.

2. His hearing is much more acute than other breeds.

3. His sense of smell is far better than any other dog possessing his other working qualities.

4. His beauty is natural and unspoiled by man.

5. He is remarkably agile and moves fast.

6. He eats very little for his size, many smaller breeds need more food.

7. His coat needs no trimming, is of medium length, not long enough to collect burrs, etc., nor too short to give insufficient protection against wet and cold.

8. He does not tire easily, he can keep moving at a steady trot almost endlessly.

9. Criminals fear Alsatians, and quickly lose courage when they encounter one.

10. He has terrific strength and can overpower an opponent very easily.

APPENDIX

GERMAN-ENGLISH TERMS

The following list (with their abbreviations) are words to be found quite frequently in German pedigrees, etc.

Abzeichen (A)—Markings, or shadings.
Ahnentafel—Pedigree.
Alter—Age.
Alterklasse (A.K.)—Adult Class.
Angekort—Certified suitable for breeding.
Augen—Eyes.
Bahndiensthund (B.D.H.)—Railroad service dog.
Befriedigend (B)—Fair, satisfactory.
Behaarung—Coat.
Besitzer—Owner.
Bindenhund (B.L.H.)—Blind leading dog.
Diensthund (D.H.)—Working dog in service.
Fahrtenhund (F.H.)—Field Trial Trailing dog.
Gang—Gait.
Geschlecht—Sex.
Geworfen—Whelped.
Herdengebrauchshund (H.G.H.)—Herding dog.
Hundin (H)—Bitch.
Jugend—Youth.
Jugenklasse (J.K.)—Youth class.
Knocken—Bone.
Kriegshund (KrH)—War dog.
Korzucht—Good Breeding qualities.
Langhaarig—Long Haired.
Leistungsieger (L.S.)—Field Trial Champion.
Polizeihund (P.H.)—Police dog.
Rude (R)—Male Dog.
Sanitatshund (S.H.)—Red Cross or medical corps dog.
Schutzhund (SchH)—Protection dog.
Schwarzgelb (sg)—Black and tan.
Schwarzgrau (sg)—Black and grey.
Sieger (S)—Champion dog.
Silbergrau (sigr)—Silver grey.
Sportklasse (SpK)—Sporting class.
Suchhund (SuchH)—Sentry and trailing dog.
Vater—Sire.
Verein—Club.
Vorzuglich (V)—Excellent.
Zotthaarig—Shaggy coat.

Zuchtbuch-nummer (SZ-NR)—Stud book number.
Zuchter (Z)—Breeder.
Zuchtrufung (Zpr)—Approved for breeding.